IN THIS ISSUE

PIVOT Magazine

Founder and President
Jason Miller

Editor-in-Chief
Chris O'Byrne

Design
JETLAUNCH.net

Advertising
Chris O'Byrne

Webmaster
Joel Phillips

Editor
Laura West

Cover Design
Debbie O'Byrne

Copyright © 2023 PIVOT

ISBN: 979-8-89079-040-8

LETTER FROM THE EDITOR

Welcome to our special edition of Pivot Magazine. This issue is dedicated to Achieve Systems, one of the most empowering organizations for business owners.

I first met Rob Raymond, president of Achieve Systems, at a lunch meeting with Jason Miller, CEO of Strategic Advisor Board. It was an incredible experience sharing a table with these two business giants. It was then that I realized Achieve Systems was the real deal.

Rob and Vanessa Raymond, along with their team of powerful alpha leaders, run Achieve Systems like a well-oiled machine. You will make valuable connections that will last you a lifetime.

But Achieve Systems is far more than just a networking group. It's a highly energized system of systems that all combine to create thriving business owners with successful businesses.

For example, they help you write and publish your book, start your own TV show, start or add a speaking business, create an effective and magnetic website, and much, much more.

The articles in this issue, many by Achieve Systems alpha leaders, will help you get a feel for what they offer you, the business leader.

When you're ready to learn more, reach out to me, directly at chris@pivotmagazines.com, and I will help you get started with the incredible Achieve Systems.

Chris O'Byrne

LETTER FROM THE DESK OF THE PRESIDENT

JASON MILLER

In 2014, two tech giants, Apple and IBM, set aside their historic rivalry to form a joint venture. The result? A series of enterprise apps that revolutionized mobile computing for businesses. This partnership generated billions in revenue and showcased how two companies, once competitors, could pool their unique strengths to create something groundbreaking.

A joint venture is a strategic alliance where two or more businesses come together to share resources, risks, and rewards in a specific project or business activity. Unlike a merger or acquisition, a joint venture allows each company to maintain its separate identity while benefiting from the partnership's collective capabilities, assets, and expertise.

In an era where rapid innovation and globalization are the norms, standing still is not an option. Businesses face many challenges, from penetrating new markets to acquiring cutting-edge technology and expertise. Joint ventures offer a viable solution to these challenges, providing a faster, less risky, and often more cost-effective way to achieve business objectives. They allow companies to leverage each other's strengths, be it market access, technology, or human capital, to gain a competitive edge.

Joint venture partnerships offer a strategic way to grow your business, increase influence, and solve complex challenges. Whether you're a business owner looking to expand your market reach or a startup aiming to accelerate product development, the right joint venture can be a game-changer. This article will delve into the intricacies of joint ventures, from their benefits and challenges to identifying the right partner, providing you with the insights you need to make an informed decision.

Joint ventures are more than just a business strategy—they catalyze transformative growth and influence in today's ever-changing business landscape.

The Basics of Joint Venture Partnerships

A joint venture is a business arrangement where two or more independent companies come together to work on a specific project or business activity. Unlike a merger, where companies combine to form a single entity, a joint venture allows each partner to maintain its individual identity. The key characteristics of a joint venture include shared ownership, shared returns and risks, and usually, a shared governance structure. The venture is often limited to a specific time frame or project, after which

the partnership may dissolve or evolve into another form.

Contractual Agreements

In this type of joint venture, the partnership is formed through contracts and agreements rather than creating a new entity. These contracts outline the roles, responsibilities, and contributions of each partner. Contractual joint ventures are often quicker to set up and offer more flexibility.

New Joint Venture Entities

The partners create a new, separate business entity to manage and govern the joint venture. This could be a new corporation, partnership, or other structure. This type of joint venture often requires more time and resources to establish but provides a clear separation between the parent companies and the new entity.

Strategic Alliances

Strategic alliances are often less formal and may not involve the creation of a new entity or contractual obligations. These are long-term partnerships where companies collaborate to achieve strategic goals. While not technically joint ventures legally, they function similarly regarding shared resources and goals.

Key Players in a Joint Venture

Partners

These are the companies that enter into the joint venture agreement. Each partner contributes resources such as capital, skills, or intellectual property and shares risks and rewards.

Stakeholders

Beyond the primary business partners, stakeholders like investors, employees, and even customers have vested interests in the joint venture's success. Their needs and expectations must be considered in the venture's strategic planning.

Management Teams

Effective governance is crucial for the success of a joint venture. A dedicated management team, often comprising members from each partner company, is responsible for the venture's day-to-day operations and strategic direction.

Understanding these basics sets the foundation for delving deeper into joint ventures' complexities and opportunities, especially for business owners looking to expand their horizons.

The Benefits of Joint Venture Partnerships

Access to New Markets

One of the most compelling benefits of a joint venture is the opportunity to access new markets. For instance, consider the case of Starbucks and Tata Global Beverages in India. Starbucks, looking to penetrate the Indian market, formed a 50/50 joint venture with Tata, a company deeply rooted in the Indian business landscape. This partnership allowed Starbucks to navigate local regulations and consumer preferences more effectively, while Tata benefited from Starbucks' global brand recognition. Within a few years, the venture successfully established hundreds of Starbucks outlets across India, proving the power of a well-executed joint venture in market penetration.

Shared Resources and Expertise

Joint ventures enable companies to pool resources and expertise, thereby amplifying their capabilities. Whether it's sharing advanced technology, specialized staff, or even distribution networks, the collaborative nature of a joint venture allows for a synergy that would be difficult to achieve independently. For example, a tech startup with groundbreaking software might lack the infrastructure to deliver its services on a large scale. By forming a joint venture with an established IT company with robust servers and a wide-reaching distribution network, both companies can benefit from each other's strengths.

Risk Mitigation

Every business venture comes with its share of risks, be it financial, operational, or market-related. Joint ventures allow for the diversification of these risks. Because both (or all) partners invest in the venture, the financial burden and associated risks are shared. This can be particularly advantageous for smaller companies or those entering unfamiliar markets. For instance, if a US-based company wants to develop a renewable energy project in a developing country, partnering with a local entity can help mitigate risks related to regulatory changes, currency fluctuations, and cultural misunderstandings.

Accelerated Growth

The combined resources and market access a joint venture provides often lead to accelerated business growth. Companies can more quickly achieve economies of scale, expand their customer base, and even diversify their product or service offerings. Take the example of the automotive industry, where companies like Toyota and BMW have entered joint ventures to speed up the development and distribution of electric vehicles. By sharing research and development costs and leveraging each other's existing dealer networks, these companies can bring new technologies to market much faster than they could independently.

In summary, joint ventures offer many benefits that can be particularly advantageous for business owners. The strategic advantages are clear, from tapping into new markets and sharing valuable resources to mitigating risks and accelerating growth. With the proper planning and partner, a joint venture can be a transformative strategy for any business looking to elevate its market position and influence.

Challenges and How to Overcome Them

Cultural and Organizational Differences

While joint ventures offer numerous benefits, they are not without challenges. One of the most common issues is the clash of cultures and organizational practices between partnering companies. These differences can manifest in various ways, from decision-making processes to communication styles and even work ethics. To overcome these challenges, it's crucial to establish a shared culture and set of values for the joint venture. Strategies for alignment can include cross-cultural training, regular joint

team meetings, and even co-location of teams for better integration. Creating a unified mission statement and set of objectives can also help align the teams and provide a common goal to work towards.

Financial Risks

Financial risks in a joint venture can range from underperformance and budget overruns to more severe issues like fraud or insolvency of one of the partners. To mitigate these risks, thorough due diligence is essential before entering into a partnership. Both parties should be transparent about their financial health and expectations for the venture. Clear financial protocols, including auditing procedures and exit strategies, can also help manage risks. Having a contingency fund and agreeing on how unexpected costs will be handled is often advisable.

Legal Complexities

Legal challenges in joint ventures can be daunting, especially when dealing with international partnerships that involve navigating different legal systems and regulations. The importance of a well-drafted contract cannot be overstated. This contract should outline the structure of the joint venture, the roles and responsibilities of each partner, the distribution of profits and losses, and procedures for dispute resolution. Given the complexities, seeking legal advice from professionals experienced in joint ventures and, if applicable, international law is highly recommended.

In conclusion, while joint ventures offer a robust growth and market penetration strategy, they come with their own challenges. However, these challenges can be effectively managed with careful planning, due diligence, and the right strategies for alignment, financial management, and legal compliance. This makes joint ventures a viable and often lucrative option for businesses looking to expand their influence and reach.

Identifying the Right Partner

Alignment of Goals and Values

Identifying the right partner is perhaps the most critical step in forming a successful joint venture. The alignment of goals and values between the partnering companies is crucial for several reasons. First, it ensures that both parties are working towards the same objectives, reducing the likelihood of conflicts and misunderstandings down the line. Second, shared values often lead to a more cohesive working relationship, which can be invaluable in navigating the challenges that inevitably arise. Finally, when goals and values are aligned, both companies can leverage each other's strengths more effectively, leading to a more productive and successful venture. To ensure alignment, open and honest discussions about each company's long-term objectives, risk tolerance, and cultural norms are essential before entering into an agreement.

Due Diligence

Due diligence is the comprehensive appraisal of a business or individual to establish facts and assess risk before signing a contract. When considering a joint venture, this involves researching potential partners thoroughly. Look into their financial stability, reputation in the market,

expertise, and any other factors crucial for the venture's success. This may involve scrutinizing financial statements, conducting background checks, and even visiting their operations if feasible. The aim is to gather all the information needed to make an informed decision. For business owners, this step is particularly crucial as a wrong partnership can not only stall growth but can also harm the reputation and financial health of your established business.

Negotiating Terms

Once you've identified a suitable partner and conducted due diligence, the next step is to negotiate the terms of the joint venture. The goal should be to create a win-win agreement that benefits both parties. Key terms to negotiate include the structure of the venture, financial contributions from each party, division of profits and losses, governance and management, and exit strategies. It's often helpful to involve legal and financial advisors in these negotiations to ensure that all bases are covered and the agreement is mutually beneficial. Remember, the best joint ventures are those where both parties feel they have something significant to gain and are committed to each other's success.

By paying careful attention to these aspects—alignment of goals and values, due diligence, and thoughtful negotiation—you increase the likelihood of forming a joint venture that is both successful and synergistic. For business owners looking to expand their influence and operational capacity, choosing the right partner can make all the difference between a joint venture that thrives and one that fails.

In today's rapidly evolving business landscape, joint venture partnerships offer a strategic avenue for growth, market penetration, and innovation. As we've explored, these partnerships come with a host of benefits, including access to new markets, shared resources and expertise, risk mitigation, and accelerated growth. However, they are not without challenges. Cultural and organizational differences, financial risks, and legal complexities can pose significant hurdles. Yet, these challenges can be effectively managed with proper planning, due diligence, and the right partner.

The alignment of goals and values is crucial for a successful partnership, as is conducting thorough due diligence to assess the suitability and reliability of potential partners. Once a partner is chosen, negotiating a win-win situation for both parties is the final step in laying the groundwork for a successful joint venture.

So why is now the best time to consider a joint venture for your business? The answer lies in the current business climate, characterized by rapid technological advancements, globalization, and increasing competition. These factors make it more challenging than ever for businesses to maintain a competitive edge. A well-executed joint venture can provide the boost needed to overcome these challenges, offering a faster, less risky, and often more cost-effective way to achieve your business objectives.

If you're looking to expand your market reach, diversify your product offerings, or simply accelerate your business growth, a joint venture could be the solution you've been searching for. Don't let opportunities pass you by; take steps now to explore how a joint venture can propel your business to new heights.

In a world where standing still is moving backward, seizing a joint venture's strategic advantage could be your business's catalyst for transformative growth and lasting success.

Jason Miller

JETLAUNCH
PUBLISHING

JETLAUNCH Publishing is for the growth-focused entrepreneur who wants to take their business to the next level by leveraging the power of a book. We take you from idea to a best-selling book to a fully automated business.

Find out how we can help you achieve that dream!

RAPIDLY GROW YOUR BUSINESS
with a bestselling book, course, and much more

Three Incredible Book Packages, Plus Exciting Extras

IGNITE **SIGNATURE** **APEX** **Add-Ons**

A better way to engage your customers

Your Customers Love Books

Unlike ads and email, they don't just throw them away. They're more likely to keep your book on their desk or bookshelf—right where they can see it every day.

Even if they never finish your book, you stay in their mind as someone who provides value and whom they can trust.

Engage your best customers with a book today!

jetlaunchpublishing.com

What People Are Saying

"Chris and his team at JETLAUNCH did an amazing job with my latest book. I loved the professional design, and everyone on the team was friendly and helpful. I highly recommend using JETLAUNCH for all of your book needs. They are a joy to work with!"

– Dr. Joe Vitale

"Their customer support is lightning fast, the quality of their work is ON FIRE. If you want a book designed—use JETLAUNCH and IGNITE your project!"

John Lee Dumas

"JETLAUNCH is the real deal! They do not disappoint! Their design and communication skills are OVER THE TOP!"

Wendy Bryant

We are ready to help double your revenue.

Call Us: 520-561-0711

Email Us: chris@jetlaunch.net

TURNING PIROUETTES INTO PROFITS: HOW A DANCER BECAME A BUSINESS MAVEN

VANESSA RAYMOND

Chris O'Byrne:

Can you tell me a little about your childhood and share a story you feel is important to who you've become today?

Vanessa Raymond:

I love this question because I always say I had a charmed childhood. I grew up in a super supportive family. I was born and raised in South Africa. My mom is an entrepreneur.

She has a computer business that she grew. My dad is an electrical engineer and a crazy hobbyist who did a ton of things. When people asked, "What does your dad do for a living?" It was hard to describe because he was a college lecturer, tech wizard, musician, pilot, etc. He did all these things. I also have an older brother who I'm very close with.

I grew up in a very versatile house. My grandmother lived with us. She was a piano and singing teacher. I grew up with a lot of music and was very passionate about dancing as a child. Whenever people would ask me, "What do you want to do when you grow up?" I responded that I wanted to be a dancer. That's all I ever wanted to do. Of course, they'd look at me and say, "No, really. A real job. What do you really want to do?"

Fortunately, I was always supported by my parents in my dreams of being a performer. I was very blessed to go to college for musical theater. I graduated as a musical theater major. Later, I also went to beauty school and did that as well because it was another passion of mine.

As far as stories go, I went through many trials and tribulations in the performance world. These challenges led to what are now some of my most beneficial attributes in the world of entrepreneurship. Because as you know, all athletes, anyone who plays an instrument, or anyone who's very passionate and serious about anything, must work hard at it. Those people understand the perseverance and tenacity it takes to make that happen.

Additionally, I grew up in a very small industrial town in South Africa. Performing wasn't a career option because there was no opportunity. So, the whole idea of that didn't make sense to most people. However, I believe that holding on to my dreams and having the support of my family is what led me to pursue my dreams. Ultimately, I left the country because of it. I wanted to go further, do more, and dream bigger.

The performance industry is what brought me to the United States, and I did live my dream. Then, of course, everything else sprouted and moved on from there.

Chris O'Byrne:

What was the transition of going from being a professional dancer/performer in the entertainment industry to starting your first business?

Vanessa Raymond:

This is interesting. I never really understood that I've always been an entrepreneur. I graduated college as a musical theater major and started performing full-time but after going to beauty school part-time and graduated, I started my own mobile beauty business, which was my first business. I never saw it as a business because it was just something else I was passionate about. But that's really where it all started.

At that time, I didn't think of it as me being an entrepreneur and growing a business. It was just me doing what I love and serving people like we do as entrepreneurs.

Eventually, I reached a point in my performance career where I realized my body was tired and I was getting older. In addition to the performance and beauty industries, I've always been very passionate about the fitness industry as well. My dad was a bodybuilder, and I grew up going to the gym. As a dancer, I was also required to do additional training to stay in shape. In 2003 I got my Pilates certification and then went on to get my yoga, personal trainer, and kettlebell certifications.

I was trying to figure out how I could step off the stage and do something else that I love. Because I was a performer, I was traveling a lot. I really wanted a child; I wanted a family. Therefore, I wanted to do something that allowed me to be more grounded and stationary to pursue my dreams of having a family. That was my big push toward starting my own fitness business.

I lived in Las Vegas at the time. I'd been working in a Pilates studio there when I wasn't on the road performing. I made a friend, and we started our own Pilates and personal training business. Neither of us knew what we were doing. It proved to be difficult. That's how I found Achieve Systems, which is the next part of the story. It was a matter of necessity.

It was difficult because it was almost like an identity shift. Until that point, I identified as a performer. I was doing what I loved and was passionate about. I always said, "Dancing isn't what I do; it's who I am." Stepping off stage was difficult, but it led to more amazing things, growth, and a whole new world.

Chris O'Byrne:

How did you and Rob Raymond meet?

Vanessa Raymond:

About 8 months into running my fitness business, my partner and I realized we were not making it. We were struggling. We didn't know how to get clients in the door. We'd been networking and doing all the "things", but we weren't really business minded. We didn't have a plan.

We went online and looked for "fitness business help" on Google. Up popped this conference that was going to be in Las Vegas, and it was the Achieve Systems conference. That is where I met Rob. He sat down with me for a one-on-one meeting. Robert, as you know already, is a huge visionary. He blew my mind in that meeting because I had not seen any of the opportunities or possibilities he laid out. When I sat down with him and told him what I was doing, he immediately had several amazing ideas for me to expand my growth and expand the business. Of course, he also guided us toward the systems we need in our business to succeed.

I was immediately impressed. I ended up joining Achieve, but it took me a while because I was very skeptical. Everything sounded too good to be true.

At the time I joined, Robert was also doing a lot of conventions. He had a fitness equipment manufacturing business at the time, and he was exhibiting at conventions all the time. This was back in 2008 and 2009. Being the creator I was, I had some workout DVDs and programs I was selling online. I also had a course that I created. I had a three-ring binder with DVDs and CDs. This was before we had all this great technology. He asked me to exhibit and sell my products in his booth, which I did. We spent a lot of time together going to these conventions, and the rest is history.

Chris O'Byrne:

You achieved your dreams, which is beautiful.

Vanessa Raymond:

Multiple times. The first time was going to musical theater college. The second was going to beauty school. Dream number three was being a successful performer and performing in the United States or London. Then, I dreamed of having a family and a successful business, and I did that. It's been amazing. It's been quite a ride.

Chris O'Byrne:

What's next for you?

Vanessa Raymond:

That's an interesting question because I love what I'm doing now. I love the growth that I'm experiencing in this whole process. Being an Achieve member has always been about building and growing my own business. However, in the meantime, I had

developed into a confidence and success coach. I work with entrepreneurs, speakers, and leaders on their confidence and self-image. This was a result of my experiences in the performance industry, fitness industry, and beauty industry brought together.

In the last year, I've made a conscious decision to be more active as a leader in Achieve Systems because most of my clientele ultimately comes straight from Achieve. So, it's been wonderful to team up with Rob in an even bigger way and help support him in the growth of this organization, which is expanding quickly in wonderful ways. It's been very rewarding to support him and be more active as an Achieve leader because that also feeds my business. They work together synergistically.

For now, my focus is really on the growth of Achieve and helping by supporting the

members and ensuring everyone has what they need for their growth and expansion.

Chris O'Byrne:

This is a very good definition of a leader, and your growth has been significant. How did Achieve come into existence?

Vanessa Raymond:

I love this story. I've heard Rob tell it a few times. He started Achieve in the early 90s, I believe. Rob also has an interesting background doing numerous different things. He's always been into sports and exercise. He was an exercise science and business major. He was passionate about the fitness industry when he started, and like me, started his own fitness business. When he moved back to Colorado, he started a mobile training business, which coincidentally, as he tells the story, grew within two years to gross over a million.

He's always been a very smart businessman. He recognized how many gyms, personal training facilities, and personal trainers were closing their doors and how many were doing part-time jobs because they couldn't make a living in this industry. Everyone in the fitness and wellness industry does what they do because they're passionate about it and want to help people. As fitness professionals, we get certifications, learn our craft, and get very good at it, but nobody shows us how to run a business. When you become a beautician, esthetician, personal trainer, physical therapist, or anything in the health and wellness realm, they teach you your craft but don't teach you how to be good at business.

Rob looked at that and had this epiphany that he wanted to help other trainers be successful. That's how it started. He started by just helping personal trainers and showing them how they could grow a business, what they needed to do, what they needed to be, and what systems they needed to have in place.

When I met him in 2008 and went to that conference, it was already pretty huge. And there were hundreds and hundreds of trainers and gym owners. And then, in 2011, When Rob and I decided things got serious between us, I moved to Colorado. That's when we re-branded the company. It used to be called Achieve Fitness Systems. We re-branded to Achieve Systems and moved into the whole health and wellness industry.

We opened a nutrition division, a wellness division, a therapy division, and all these different health and wellness divisions. He grew that. About three years ago, we decided to open our doors to all entrepreneurs. That's the evolution of where that came from. But it really sparked from him wanting to help others. His motive's always been to help others grow successful businesses and be as successful as he has been.

Chris O'Byrne:

I figured that out pretty fast when I first met him. It was all about how he could help.

Vanessa Raymond:

It is his passion. He lives for that. He always says to me, "I don't need the money. It is about the people. Our members' success is our success because the more successful our people are, the more successful we are." It has always been about that for him.

Chris O'Byrne:

Again, real leadership. That's the heart of it. What is it that makes Achieve so unique and incredible?

Vanessa Raymond:

Honestly, Chris, I cannot say that I have come across any other organization that incorporates all the aspects we incorporate in Achieve Systems. Some organizations do similar things, but it's only parts and pieces of what we do—not the whole gamut.

Rob has done a very good job adding important components throughout the years. Every time he recognized a need in the marketplace or the industry, he would add a solution to that specific need. We've come to a point where when people ask me what Achieve is, I cringe because it is such a giant to explain to others without them feeling "fire-hosed" haha.

To put it simply, we support entrepreneurs and business owners, providing them with resources and revenue streams to grow their businesses. Anything and everything you can think of that a business owner needs to up-level their business no matter where they are, whether they're a startup, have been in business for two years and are struggling, or they're thriving and doing seven or eight figures.

Rob preaches seven-plus revenue streams in a business to create wealth. If you want to create wealth or a seven or eight-figure business, you need seven-plus revenue streams. He also teaches that we want to create our revenue streams. That's what we do. We help our members create these revenue streams.

We have resources to help them author books, create education and bring it to market, brand themselves properly, invent products, start a magazine, start their networking event system, start a TV show, create apps, etc. We have a speaker division because we recognize that if you're going to grow as a business owner, you need to speak, be out there, and be visible. We have live events, conferences, virtual events, happy hours, mastermind calls, and more. We also have a division for kids.

We're growing and adding constantly. There's always new stuff, new marketing plans. He's a great proponent of staying up to date with what's happening in the marketing world because so many marketing coaches out there teach good stuff, but it's outdated.

At the same time, we're also a support system and give our members accountability, so they keep moving forward and don't quit. It's tough for everybody, especially those first two or three years in any business. Part of our job is keeping entrepreneurs moving forward and not quitting, keeping them on the path and moving forward.

Chris O'Byrne:

Being an Achieve member myself, I see and experience the insight. I know the incredible wealth of resources, help, and wisdom Achieve Systems and its members have to offer.

Vanessa Raymond:

We are very proud of the leadership team we have put together. As a membership program, it's ever-evolving. Through the years, we've had some amazing leaders, but our current team is the strongest leadership team we've ever had. Partnering with SAB and other larger organizations has been amazing because it offers more resources for our leaders and members to thrive.

Chris O'Byrne:

As one of the owners of the Strategic Advisory Board (SAB), it was such an honor to become part of your team and provide one more way to help Achieve Systems grow. Your vision is huge, but you're making it real, which is something that you don't see very often. You see people with a big vision, but they cannot carry through and make it happen. Now you have this thriving, huge organization of business owners, all these people who have come together to learn from you and your team and to learn from each other. You also do a very good job of encouraging people to contribute their wisdom and experience and help others because, regardless of their annual revenue, everybody has something to offer, and everybody can learn something from somebody else. That has really impressed me about Achieve Systems.

Vanessa Raymond:

I appreciate that, Chris. Yes. It's been amazing to watch Rob and his team. He's a very high-energy human being, and he's big on action. That's why he's been able to create what he's created because he takes immediate action. Sometimes, I'm like, *Okay, that was maybe a little premature* or whatever, but that's the point.

He works incredibly fast. Nobody can keep up with him. I think that makes this organization extraordinary because he is an implementer. The idea comes, and it's been implemented before you even know it. I think that's part of what the success of this company is about—implementation. We sometimes have to adjust as we go along because Rob launches, and then he adjusts. But that is where success comes from because many of us tend to procrastinate. He doesn't.

Also, it's that growth mindset of knowing that you launch something, adjust, and if it fails, you change things or you just move

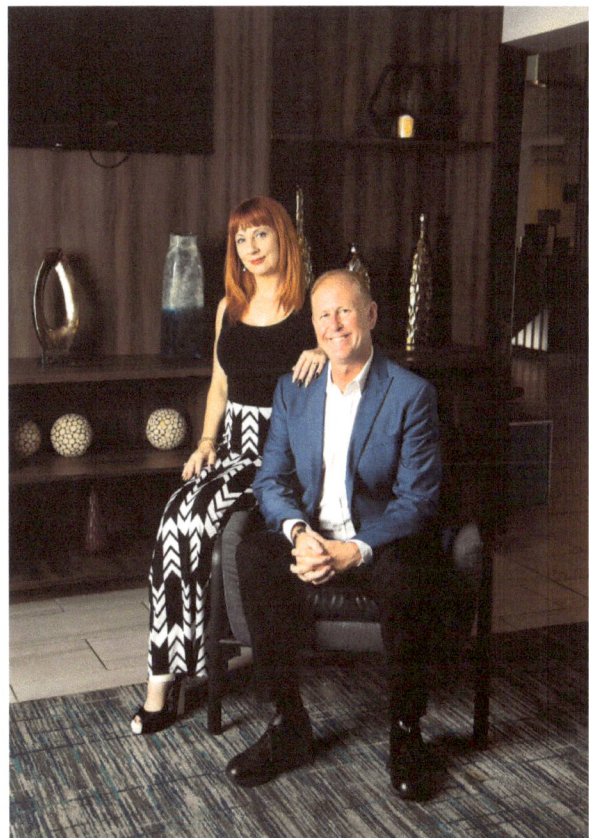

on to the next thing. That's part of being an entrepreneur and a business owner. He is a good example to the community, and they follow him. I've learned a lot from him, too. I'm trying to be that same example. I'm watching him every day, kicking butt, and it inspires me to do the same. It's leading by example. Everything we do: We test. We try. Then, when we know it works we bring it to the community.

Chris O'Byrne:

What are the big plans for Achieve? What's coming down the pike?

Vanessa Raymond:

We look forward to growing our community substantially. We want to be known as the world's largest community of entrepreneurs and business owners. We have spread our wings to other countries already. We've had a member in Australia. We have a couple of members in the UK. We are in Africa. We want to be internationally known.

We are also working toward being a publicly traded company. And just along the way, being the best support we can be, letting entrepreneurs know that there is support and that we are here to fill those shoes if needed.

One of the things that I didn't mention is Rob's vision to make business support available to struggling entrepreneurs because the people who struggle can't afford the business coaches. He wanted to help, and that's why it's a membership program. It's a super affordable model for entrepreneurs to have the support and resources without paying an arm and a leg.

We all need support at times, but we want to get them there, where they can afford the deeper dive with the bigger, larger coach or whatever they need later on. But many companies are lost and struggling and don't know how to get where they need to go without making a huge investment upfront. And so that's the other part of this vision.

Chris O'Byrne:

And at this point, there's no way you won't reach that vision because you never give up. And if you don't give up, you can't *not* reach it. It has to happen. What is one of the most important lessons you've learned as an entrepreneur?

Vanessa Raymond:

As a speaker, one thing I talk about a lot is showing up—showing up no matter what. One of the biggest pitfalls for most entrepreneurs is we're not visible because we're so entrenched in the everyday hustle. We're doing so many things that we feel we need to do just to keep our businesses running. In the end, that visibility factor is so huge. We can't be the "best-kept secret" if we want to be successful.

Aside from showing up and being visible, my main lesson has been not giving up when times get tough. This is a lesson I learned in the performance industry. When you go to dance class, step into a dojo, get on the field, or show up wherever it is as an athlete, there's no way out. There's no giving up. It's about discipline. If people—and entrepreneurs—were more accountable to themselves, they would be more successful. It's about doing the grind, keeping going, not stopping, not quitting. We all fall. We have to get up again. Understanding that those failures are not failures; they're learning experiences. That's the next step to the next thing. Just keep going. Keep showing up day after day after day. Don't quit because the people who are successful are the ones who just keep on going no matter what!

Action Steps

Reevaluate your revenue streams: Inspired by Vanessa's emphasis on having multiple revenue streams, take a moment to assess your current income channels. Are they diversified enough? If not, brainstorm additional revenue streams that align with your core business and start taking steps to implement them.

Invest in personal development: Vanessa's journey shows the importance of continuous learning and personal growth. Whether it's getting a new certification, attending industry conferences, or simply reading up on the latest trends, invest in yourself to become more versatile and adaptable in your business.

Prioritize visibility and networking: Vanessa's success in multiple fields highlights the importance of being visible and well-connected. Consider ways to increase your business's visibility, whether it's through social media, public speaking, or partnerships. Also, don't underestimate the power of networking; attend industry events and join organizations that can help you meet potential clients or collaborators.

About the Author

Vanessa is a seasoned international speaker, author, confidence and success coach, as well as a multiple business owner.

After performing professionally on stages around the world for over a decade, Vanessa pursued a career in the fitness and wellness industry. She focuses on helping people improve their quality of life by becoming healthier and reducing pain. Vanessa understands the connection between movement and mental-emotional toughness for success in both life and business.

As an educator, Vanessa has created multiple national CEC-approved education programs that have impacted the success of thousands. Drawing from her experience in various industries, she created the Self-Image and Confidence Coaching Certification Program, known as The Victory Factor.

Vanessa is also a successful entrepreneur and serves as the Executive Leader and Director of Education for Achieve Systems, one of the largest health and wellness communities and coaching support systems in the industry. She is a devoted wife and mother of three.

Vanessa helps entrepreneurs, speakers, and leaders improve their confidence, create meaningful relationships, and establish a powerful business image, enabling them to achieve success personally, professionally, and financially.

Confidence

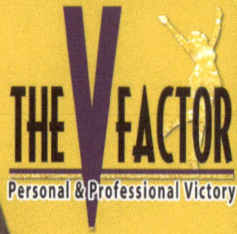

Power Confidence
Platinum Coaching Program

Vanessa's book is available on Amazon

POWER Confidence
Your Ultimate Guide to Unstoppable Self Confidence
Vanessa Raymond

- Bring in high profile clients and increase your client retention by knowing how to show up as the expert with a powerful presence

- Stand out in the crowd in a sea of distracion, on the phone, on video at networking events and on stage

- Show up in an approachable and professional way by communicating effectively

- Be catapulted forward in your success and generate revenue with more ease

Hire Vanessa to:

Speak at your next event

Train your employees and leaders to be better communicators with her "Workplace Empowerment Program"

Certify you as a Self-Image Coach

Contact Vanessa:
📞 **720-317-4594**

More Information:
www.victoryinbiz.com.com
Vanessa@VictoryFactor.com

6 SECRETS TO MAGNETIZING YOUR AUDIENCE FOR BUSINESS SUCCESS

VANESSA RAYMOND

You walk into the room, and all eyes are on you. You're standing tall, have a smile on your face, and everyone is intently listening to what you have to say... and then you wake up. Most of us have fantasized about the ability to make heads turn, but how many of us can actually command a room?

Why is it that when certain people walk into a room, you can't help but notice them right away? You just have to look—and stare. Is it his good looks or his Armani suit? Maybe it was her Prada shoes or her Versace dress?

I guarantee you it has very little to do with the clothes he is wearing or her shoes.

We get brainwashed into believing these people are just born with that stunning flair and magnetic presence—that "It" factor- the elusive thing we can't quite put our finger on. Most celebrities have it; most successful people have it.

The thing is that you also can be noticed and make an astonishing *first impression.* Don't think you need to be born with it or that it is only reserved for the rich and the famous. Believe me, most people who have this presence and radiate irresistible magnetism are aware of it and constantly work at it.

In business, the more we can raise our awareness of how we show up, the better our chances of being successful at magnetizing our ideal clients. You need to own your worth and show up with total confidence in yourself and what you offer. Otherwise, how do you expect anyone else to believe in you and to engage in your product or service?

We are vibrational beings, and we transmit energy all the time. Some of us project energy at higher frequencies than others. These are the vibrations that people pick up and notice about you within the first few moments of meeting you. Before you have even had an opportunity to say something, the chances are good that the other person already made some sort of assessment about you. They already got a first impression within seconds of seeing you.

Take a moment and think about the impression you want to leave in the minds of those prospects and clients you interact with daily.

The principles I am about to share with you can be applied to stepping on stage, walking into a networking event or a job interview, and even how you present yourself on a video call or even on the phone while working with clients and handling your sales calls.

Elevating your magnetic presence is about consciously projecting positive energy.

You can quickly start implementing a few principles for greater business and life success.

Awareness

Self-awareness of how you present yourself is the first and most important secret to making great first impressions and ensuring you linger in their minds long after you leave. An acute awareness of your good posture and your body language is what is going to make all the difference.

Posture

Great posture goes a long way. Your posture, the way you hold your body, can dictate how others perceive you. It is true that our emotions often influence our posture. If you feel intimidated or shy, you might drop your chin, hunch your shoulders forward, and avoid eye contact. This would be a dead giveaway that you are uncomfortable, and chances are that others will feel just as uncomfortable in your presence.

The posture of a self-confident, poised person is upright and proud with chin lifted, chest open, and quite often a smile. This is the person who will get noticed right away.

The truth is that even when you are feeling slightly intimidated, if you can master the posture and poise of someone feeling self-assured and in control, you can use this posture and immediately start looking and feeling more confident. You will instantly have a more confident presence. You can affect your mood or emotions by simply changing your posture.

Spend a few minutes in front of the mirror and make yourself aware of what this great, self-confident posture looks and feels like.

Intention

Once you are aware that you have the power to use your posture to position yourself as a more self-confident person, all you need is the intention for others to see you that way. Decide to make an impressive entrance and leave everyone wondering, "Who is this person?" Once you have the intention, your body will find it easy to turn on that unmistakable posture, poise, and presence you practiced in the mirror before.

Graciousness

Life has become a rat race, and we get caught up in our heads, not paying much attention to the people around us. One of the greatest secrets to being remembered in a positive light is to be gracious. We so often get into the habit of asking, "How are you?" but how often do we pay attention to the answer?

How often do you compliment someone or simply extend a friendly smile?

By being sincerely interested in the other person, by greeting and smiling genuinely, you can be sure to get noticed and remembered and make an impression.

Eye contact

How often have you gone on a date or sat in a meeting where you felt you were not included in the conversation or the other person was distracted and uninterested?

By maintaining eye contact with the person you are conversing with, you assure them you are totally engaged and interested, and they immediately feel important and included. If you are talking to a group, make eye contact with everyone there if possible because you will make them feel included and significant. Connect with every section of the room when you have an audience of hundreds or maybe thousands. This also establishes your confident presence and control of the conversation.

Sincerity

You can do all this—have the self-awareness, the great posture, the right intention, be gracious, and maintain eye contact—but if there is no genuine sincerity behind your actions, people will look right through you.

By practicing these principles and utilizing these few guidelines, you will definitely be noticed and remembered. It doesn't cost anything, and once you feel comfortable and confident in your own skin with your new posture, poise, and presence, you will be remembered as someone with that "special something"—that victory factor!

FOR EVERY BUSINESS & BUDGET

Looking for a website design firm or D.I.Y. platform that can help you build a visually stunning and effective online brand? Look no further than our expert team. At Proshark, we help you build a customized website that meets your unique needs and goals and converts visitors to customers.

PROSHARK SITES

INNOVATION DESIGNED TO INSPIRE

www.proshark.com

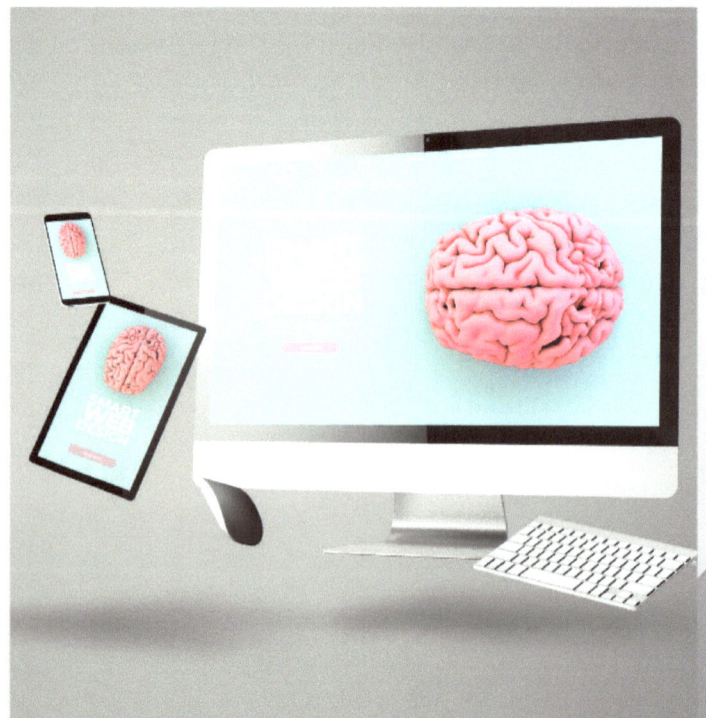

NONPROFIT OF THE MONTH: EMPTYING THE JAIL

WILL BLACK

Have you ever seen the *Andy Griffith Show*? They have three jail cells for the entire town, and all are empty except one that is often used by the town drunk, Otis, who stumbles into his cell, locks himself in, hangs up the key, and sleeps it off. In the morning, he lets himself out again.

This is the dream of the Coastal Jail Ministry—emptying the jails as best they can. Here's the *wow* moment: 80% of the men and women that go through their program *never see the inside of a jail again!* They flip the national rate of recidivism on its head.

If you were to ask them what makes it so special, how they achieve these fantastic numbers that would be the envy of any rehabilitation program in the country, you'd never hear of them. Dog programs, conjugal visits, and farm programs get all the media attention, but this is a ministry. They get to the root and heart of the matter. They make men and women take a real look at themselves and see the error, the sin in their own hearts. They meet God there, and that changes them forever.

One example is of a convicted murderer. He did it. He was guilty. He knew it. Everyone knew it. He confessed it. But jail doesn't have safe places where you can let your guard down. The men and women inside always, *always* have their guard up. And yet... at the end of classes, if you have done the work, you graduate. You're recognized by peers and the chaplains. You're given a Bible, and not a cheap one, but a fairly expensive, large study Bible.

It was this convicted murder's turn. He passed and had done well. He was congratulated, they shook his hand, he was applauded, and given his Bible.

And he clutched it to his body and wept.

He wept openly. He sobbed choking on air in gasps. All the other men could see it, and this known murderer didn't care and simply choked out the words, "I've never had something like this." It wasn't the book, or the expense. It was the Word and the training and how it would change the rest of his life, even though the rest of his life would all be behind bars. He knows that if this had happened only two years earlier, maybe things would have been different. He didn't have it earlier, but he has it now.

This ministry once came under fire when it was said they wouldn't minster to other faiths, but that is just not true. They will minister to anyone. What they won't do is preach a different message. Sadly, they were removed from the jail. Still, they continue and work with the ministry of those coming out of the jail who need counseling, jobs, support, and a brother in Christ, until they can get back into the jail. Unfortunately, faith is under heavy attack these days, but they will not bend the knee or change their message.

If you have a business and would like to support these chaplains and help empty the jails, one Bible at a time, click below:

DOING GOOD IS
GOOD BUSINESS

UNLEASHING YOUR INNER VOICE TO TRANSFORM YOUR BUSINESS AND YOUR LIFE

CATHY REILLY

Choose a story from your childhood that you feel was important in becoming who you are today.

When I was in high school, I had a joke played on me that had a profound effect on me. I wouldn't recognize the significance until much later. When I was a freshman at a new high school—new to the scene, shy, introverted, and struggling to use my voice and even find my identity. I grew up in a house that had one phone that everyone shared and used. It was located on the main floor in the kitchen. With three siblings and my parents, there were times when we had to wait in line to use the phone. As a typical teenage girl, I spent a fair amount of time talking on the phone with my best friend. What's funny about those times is that when you wanted to communicate with your friends, you hoped the other person was at home and they answered the phone. Talking on the phone was a big deal and a coordinated effort. As you can imagine, a popular topic of conversation was boys we were crushing on. The phone itself was located in the kitchen, and it had that long cord I had to pull around into the next room to have what I thought was a private conversation.

Dinner time was a sacred time in my household, and we broke bread together every night. One night at dinner, my father told me a boy called. For the sake of this story, I'll call him Joe. With great enthusiasm, I said, "Really?" You see, I had been crushing on Joe and talking to my girlfriends about him. I really hoped he'd ask me to the dance.

"What did he say?" I asked my father. He replied, "I don't know. I'm not your secretary." I said, "Okay, did he leave a number?" My father responded curtly, "Nope." Not knowing how to respond, I got on the phone with my girlfriend and asked, "What do I do? What do I do?" Collectively, we devised a plan for me to talk to him the next day at school. I would gain the courage to go talk to him if he didn't talk to me first. Great plan—or so I thought.

The next day, we got to school, the morning passed, and no conversation with him. I were at lunch, whispering with my friends,

building up the courage to talk to him. Here I go...

He was standing by his locker collecting his books with his friends. I walked over and said, "Hey, Joe!" I fumbled through my words. "Ummm, having a good day? Hope you're having a good day." More fumbling of my words. "I heard you called my house last night. Did you want to ask me something? What did you want to talk about?"

He looked me up and down as if in slow motion, lifted the corner of his lip as if he tasted something bitter, and said, "I didn't call you. I *wouldn't* call you." He let out a huge belly laugh, scoffed, turned around, slammed his locker and walked away with his crew. My heart landed on the ground at my feet. I was humiliated. I thought, *Oh, my God. What did I do wrong? How did I get this so wrong?* When the school day ended, I rushed home in humiliation.

That night, the family was gathered for dinner. Still humiliated and massively confused, I said to my father, "Hey, Dad. I talked to Joe today, and he said he didn't call me. Are you sure about the call? Can you remember who called?" Dad paused and started to laugh. After a few moments of silence, I asked in a confuzzled state (combination of confused and puzzled) "What?"

Dad laughed again and said he was just kidding. The boy never called. He heard me talking about him on the phone and thought it would be funny to spin my wheels a bit. I was humiliated not once but twice—by the boy and then by my father. This joke stayed with me for a long time until I finally grasped the lesson.

When I became an entrepreneur and established my business, I never quite got past a certain threshold. It felt like something was holding me back. I often wondered what was the missing piece, so I started doing some digging, researching, and self-reflection. I am part nerd, have a degree in psychology. and get excited to dig into neuroscience. I applied all that to rejection. I found that there are many reasons why people hold themselves back, and many more why people don't succeed. It's often their fear of rejection—and that was me. It was vital to me to find the answer to the question: *How do I get over the fear of rejection?* Once I grasped how to shift my mindset around rejection, how to eliminate it from holding me back, my business showed up differently. I showed up differently.

The key to understanding rejection is that it's not personal. The rejection isn't about me; it's about the other person, the person saying no. People say no for a few reasons—there is a lack of understanding or insufficient information, timing, or misalignment of core values. Perhaps they don't have a clear understanding of what's being offered and therefore feel it's not for them. It's not personal.

When I applied that to Joe, I could understand how, when I approached him about something he didn't do, he was confused. A confused mind struggles. I tied his response to me personally, when it had everything to do with the situation, not me. This rejection stuck with me for a long time and impacted my business. When I was finally able to flip the switch and compare making an offer in my business to making an offer for gum, it took the personal aspect out of it. When we offer gum to our friends, we don't think twice when they say no. We know it's not personal. We must transfer this to our business. So, my philosophy now is SWSWSW: Some will. Some won't. So what? Someone's waiting.

Years ago, I read this great book called *Go For NO!* It bolstered my new perspective on rejection and initiated the 100-day no challenge that I now do and live by. If you go to my website, you will find a 100-day no challenge form you can download today. With this small shift in perspective on rejection, I now go for the no. There's something juicy about getting that no. It's liberating. And then, of course, you reward yourself for getting the no because the more no's you get, the closer you get to yes. As entrepreneurs, we live for the yeses.

What inspired you to start your business?

My daughter is the reason why I started my business way back when. She was born in 2005 and I started a business in 2006. I used to be a litigation paralegal and spent twenty-five years working with attorneys, litigating, and making my attorneys look good, which is not easy. But I did love the law, and I loved my job. However, I didn't like the hours.

When I was about eight months pregnant, I had a client who needed a motion filed immediately, and only two people could do it: my attorney and me. We worked until almost 11:00 p.m. on this brief because we had to finish it for a client. That was a real wake-up call because my priority as a parent will always be my family.

I decided to branch out and figure out my exit strategy from law and what I could do. Now, I'm an introvert; I'm very shy and struggle with communicating in words. I'm good at making everybody else look good, but I struggled with myself. Plus, what could I do?

I'm also part raccoon. I started a business in direct sales with jewelry, which was fabulous because I barely had to talk to anybody. I just had to put the pretties out there, and they sold themselves. It was easy and duplicatable, and I build a great team. I had a great business, but then I experienced some health crises. Then, the company without

warning, closed its doors, and I reinvented myself again, still insisting that family would be first in my life. My daughter is my inspiration.

My current business is all about self-advocacy, using your voice and speaking your truth. It shifted after all my health issues, but at the end of the day, this job allows me a true career in alignment with my values and my mission. It allows me to be present with my family, be flexible, and support my family. It's a business I created because of my daughter. Here's the thing: As a parent, she won't necessarily do what I say to do. Ultimately, she will do what I do. I'm leading by example. I'm creating a successful business, helping entrepreneurs use their voices strategically to grow their businesses, get on stages, and do all that. I'm teaching her that she can, too. She has been my number-one inspiration in everything I do.

Share some key influences or mentors who have played a significant role in your entrepreneurial journey.

The first big influence in my life and business was a gentleman by the name of Trey Malicoat, a life coach. I met him on my road to recovery. I had mentioned before that I had some health crises, and to explain a little more, I had four surgeries in five months. I went down, and I went down hard. In one of those surgeries, I nearly lost my life due to an ectopic pregnancy. I talk more about it in my book, but it came down to me being unable to pick up the phone and call for help. As I was on the road to recovery, I aspired to be a stronger version of myself—a better version. I was on a mission to learn how to be my own advocate and use my voice because I struggled repeatedly and couldn't ask for help. I just knew, there had to be a way to figure it out, and I was on that path to doing just that.

I met Trey during a course I was taking, and he asked, "When was the last time you really needed help and couldn't ask?" It wasn't difficult for me to answer because it was when I was lying on the floor in pain and couldn't pick up the phone to call for help. I was struggling with what I now call my Itty-Bitty Shitty Committee—my stinking thinking. Because of that negative self-talk, I talked myself out of asking for help. I truly felt unworthy and insignificant. I didn't want to bother anybody else, so I stayed quiet. I now know that we can't do that. We need to value ourselves to show up.

Trey and I started working together. We figured out that my Itty-Bitty Shitty Committee was holding me back. I did small things to change who I was, how I was showing up, and how I valued myself. It was vital. The more I worked with him, the more he said, "You know what? I see you taking stages." I cursed at him. I said, "There's no way I will ever take a stage. I am terrified to have a one-on-one conversation, let alone be in front of hundreds of thousands of people." Six years later, I took the stage. When I was done, I remember feeling gratitude for the opportunity to share my message to help others step into self-advocacy. It was very empowering.

I called Trey and said, "You were right. You could see it. I couldn't." And that's why I always believe in working with a coach, somebody who will see things you don't.

It's important to know you don't know what you don't know. And to have other eyes on you, whether it's personally or professionally. This helps you effectively navigate your journey in a way that's empowering and helps you get to where you want to go—faster, stronger, more powerful, and more profitable. Trey was amazing, and I still work with coaches. I've worked with Lisa Nichols, Jack Canfield, and Tony Robbins. Many people have influenced me. But Trey was the one who ignited this transition of this new version of Cathy.

What makes your business unique and valuable?

My business model is different because of my unique perspective on finding what my client needs. I don't believe in coaching individuals or speaking to organizations with a one-size-fits-all mantra. I dive deep into my client: What are their needs? What are their fears? What are their goals? What do they want to accomplish? About 20 percent of entrepreneurs fail in year two and about 50 percent of entrepreneurs fail in year five.

When working with my clients, I always ask, "What's holding you back from accomplishing your goals?" The answer is, more often than not, "Me." Entrepreneurs hold themselves back. Whether it's fear, their negative self-talk I call the Itty-Bitty Shitty Committee, or the compare and despair factor, entrepreneurs hold *themselves* back. There are small shifts, strategies, and tools they can learn that can make a huge impact in their business, and in all honestly, them personally. These small changes shift how they show up, how they converse with themselves, set goals, plan their strategic business plan, what they think they can do, and how they can use their voice—whether it's on social media, in sales conversations, or from big stages. I help clients flip the switch and show up for themselves like they show up for everyone else.

I talk a lot about self-advocacy. Originally, my business had a lot to do with personal health and wellness and how we show up for ourselves personally and give ourselves permission to ask for help. Over the years, it has morphed into working with entrepreneurs, organizations, and business leaders to advocate for their businesses alongside themselves personally so they can be seen and heard and at the end of the day, make more money.

I partner with many entrepreneurs because they truly struggle with holding themselves back. When my clients go deep into how they can make that small switch to figure out what's holding them back, everything changes. I become their biggest fan and cheerleader. In the beginning, entrepreneurs don't believe in themselves. They struggle with that. When things are going well, they feel confident; when things are going bad, they let the fear set in. So, I help them show up for themselves and cheer them on. I become their biggest advocate, their cheerleader, and I become the voice outside their head that eventually develops into that little voice inside their head that says, "You can do it!" I believe in them before they can. When you have somebody like that in your corner, you're unstoppable. That's when I know you can unleash the power of you.

What is one of the most valuable lessons you've learned as an entrepreneur?

The biggest lesson in my nearly twenty-year journey is knowing everything is figureoutable. I now know I have the tools, the resources, and the know-how to make to make success happen; I just have to dig a little.

Things are not laid out for us as entrepreneurs. We have to find the answers. I wish I would have known that. I want you to understand that whether you are new to this business or have been doing this for decades, you can figure *anything* out. Do you want to start speaking? You can figure it out. Do you want to publish a book? You can figure it out. Do you want to add a new stream of income? You can figure it out. Everything is figureoutable. Like I said before, you already have the knowledge, skill, and ability to make all the success happen. You have it. You just need to unfold it. You need to dig into it. You need to ask questions. You need to hire a coach, research, share information with your peers, and ask tons of questions. Then, you must have the courage to take the steps you need to move forward to make your next best decision.

The courage comes from also having your Fab Five. I'm sure you've heard that who you hang out with can determine your future. The same is true for a business owner. The five people you spend the most time with reflect the status of your business. Who

are the five people you spend the most time with? Are they people who lift, support, and challenge you? Are they in alignment with your mission? Are they on the same journey as you? Those are the kind of people you need to be hanging out with. If you don't have a Fab Five, find them. Find other entrepreneurs to spend time with, brainstorm with, and talk. They don't necessarily have to be in the same profession as you. For instance, I have a doctor, a lawyer, a coach, a finance person in my Fab Five. They can be anybody as long as they get you and are on the same mission as you: to grow and be successful in business.

My Fab Five and I are on a seven-figure mission—make it to a million or bust! We're doing things that make us uncomfortable and stretch us, and we're there for each other. Your Fab Five will help you. You can lean on them. You can talk to them. It's

great when you're like, "Well, I'm thinking about doing this…" and one of them will tell you, "Oh, wait, I tried that. Don't waste your money." It's like your personal board of directors for your business.

It's about having courage. It's taking that breath, facing your fears, and doing it. Whatever it is, just do it. If I had known all this twenty years ago, my business would be different. But at the end of the day, my journey led me here. We're celebrating my success, and it has been an honor and privilege to be where I am and help the people I've helped.

How have you and your business benefited from your involvement with Achieve Systems?

Achieve and Robert Raymond have been instrumental in transforming my business perspective. Robert's insights have illuminated the incredible advantages of diversifying income streams. While I initially focused on just one facet of my business, Robert's keen vision uncovered profitable layers that were hidden in my blind spot. In addition, the quarterly conferences, daily masterminds, and resources provide immense educational and networking benefits, offering exceptional value. Every business owner or entrepreneur would benefit from becoming a part of Achieve.

What does your morning routine look like?

My morning routine consists of getting up at 5:30 a.m., I call it the o'dark-thirty hour, splashing water on my face, looking at myself in the mirror, and complimenting myself. Nine times out of ten, your first thought is negative when you look in the mirror. If you're telling yourself something negative in the morning, you're starting your day on a negative note. Negativity begets negativity. I strategically compliment myself to start the day on a positive note. I teach this to my clients, too. It's super juicy, even if all you can say is, "You got this. It's going to be a great day. You can do it!"

Next is my morning meditation. I curate a specific morning meditation that combats my Itty-Bitty Shitty Committee that focuses on the activities leading me to my goals and overcomes any struggles that may impact me for the quarter. Instructions on how to curate your own medication is a chapter in my book. If you want to learn how to do it yourself, it is super powerful. It truly sets the tone for how you tackle the day and how you tackle any challenge that may come your way.

And then, from 6:00 a.m. to 7;00 a.m., I do what I call a power hour, where I get online virtually with power partners who are in my organization and doing the same activities as me. We all use social media to grow our business, but honestly, it's rough and can be a rabbit hole. So, collectively we focus on what we need to do and staying on talk: making approaches, building relationships, talking to people, and pitching ourselves. When it comes to being a speaker, I have to pitch myself and tell people how great I am. It's the business side of speaking, that little secret. My power partners and I spend an hour doing uncomfortable activities, and it just feels good to be with other people doing the same thing.

After the power hour, I work out. I energize my brain, and then I energize my body. I mix up my workouts and do triathlons, swim, bike, run, work on some form of cardio, yoga, and the rower machine. I also have a punching bag that's great for stress.

After the workout, I end my morning with breakfast, which I love. I seriously love to eat. I change it up, alternating between protein, fruit, and veggies and then hit the shower. I am at my desk meeting with clients by about 10:00 a.m. I do that every morning. That's my morning routine. I know and appreciate the fact that routine is important for an entrepreneur, as it's the cornerstone for boundaries. Boundaries are important for an entrepreneur.

What parting words of wisdom do you have for the reader?

I'd like to end with this: Your voice matters. *You* matter. As an entrepreneur, there's so much hesitation around using your voice and speaking up and having those difficult conversations. But you have everything you need right now. You are brilliant. Your business is amazing. You have so many good things moving forward. Please know you are worth it. Your voice matters, so stop talking negatively to yourself and convincing yourself that you can't do it. That's that Itty-Bitty Shitty Committee and it's time for it to sit down and be quiet.

Pay attention to that conversation going on inside your head. Have you ever thought about it? Have you ever really listened? Start thinking about it. What are you saying to yourself? As a guide, know this: If you cannot say it out loud to a grandparent or a child, you have no business saying it to yourself. Make a shift and start talking to yourself out loud. When you hear what's going on, start speaking up. You'll be shocked once you start paying attention to that.

You're so worth it. You're so amazing. You just need to believe it. So, when you're feeling negative, take a deep breath and tell your Itty-Bitty Shitty Committee to sit down and be quiet. Enough. Speak your truth; use your words. Start telling people how great you are. You are amazing. I'm not saying brag but own your space. Start using social media and talk about your success stories, how you've made an impact, and the greatness that you bring.

Write a book. I believe every entrepreneur should write a book. You have a story. Your story is a gift. Everyone needs to hear it. Start speaking from stages. Your voice can have a huge impact. And speaking from the stage is where you grow. It's uncomfortable but worth it. You're worth it. Your voice matters. We need to hear from you.

Action Steps

1. **Confront your fear of rejection**: The author's journey highlights the importance of overcoming the fear of rejection. This is a common obstacle that holds many entrepreneurs back from reaching their full potential. Consider taking a course on handling rejection or reading books that offer strategies to cope with it. Implement the SWSWSW philosophy: "Some will. Some won't. So what? Someone's waiting." This mindset can help you become more resilient and open to opportunities.

2. **Assemble your Fab Five**: The author emphasizes the value of surrounding yourself with people who uplift you and align with your mission. Take time to evaluate your current network and identify five individuals who can serve as your personal board of directors. These should be people who challenge you, support you, and are on a similar journey of growth and success. Regularly consult with them to gain different perspectives and to hold yourself accountable.

3. **Develop a strong morning routine**: The author's morning routine is designed to set a positive tone for the day, starting with self-affirmation and followed by focused work, exercise, and planning. Create your own morning routine that prepares you mentally, emotionally, and physically for the day ahead. This could include meditation, a power hour of focused work, or any other activities that energize you and align with your goals.

About the Author

Cathy Reilly is CEO of Sharing the Shine, an international speaker, and a personal leadership and mindset mastery coach. With a background in psychology, business, law, and NLP, Cathy leverages her two decades of advocacy experience to unlock human potential, navigate change, and drive success in both life and business. She firmly believes that success begins within us and our daily choices.

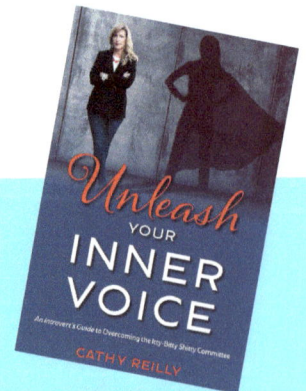

THE ROLE OF COMMUNITY IN GOO$E MAGAZINE'S SUCCESS FORMULA

CHARLIE STIVERS

Choose a story from your childhood that you feel was important in becoming who you are today.

I grew up on an Angus cattle farm in Western New Jersey. My father was a business owner, entrepreneur, and self-employed. He was also an investor, and he taught us about investing at a young age. I remember investing $25 a month in a mutual fund. When I was twenty-three, my father passed away. Luckily, he had life insurance for us seven kids. It wasn't a lot, but I wanted to honor him.

It was 1998 when he passed, right in the middle of the dotcom craze. I was in college studying tech and business. I was like Alex P. Keaton (from the TV show *Family Ties*) walking around with the business section of the newspaper. I loved reading about technology in the business section and the news. I was researching internet stocks and didn't want to blow the money I was gifted from him, so I invested half of it in the stock market and a lot of the dotcom and tech companies.

Needless to say, that was good timing. You couldn't go wrong with tech stocks in the late 90s, and I loved it so much that I became licensed as a financial professional in 2001. I then ran a financial planning practice for seventeen years.

What inspired you to start your business?

At the beginning of the pandemic lock-downs, I turned to gratitude. The positive I took from it was I got to focus on cryptocurrency. In early 2020, I bought my first Bitcoin and Ethereum, and I documented my journey on social media. Since most of us didn't have a lot of other things to do, I attracted a group. We all shared and bounced ideas off each other about cryptocurrency investing.

Toward the end of 2020, I launched cryptocurrencyforthepeople.com and then started a small community. As I was growing this, I discovered that some people wanted to hire me personally. I started a consulting part and coached people one-on-one on how to get started in crypto the right way, which is safely and confidently so that we can be profitable; from there, it grew.

Several months later, the world started opening back up. Achieve started their conferences again, and one of their speakers at a conference talked about how magazines were making a comeback. They spoke specifically about print magazines and how they can be a marketing piece that helps build credibility. *Bitcoin Magazine* was the only crypto magazine I knew because I was using it as a part of my research. The idea popped into my head that another crypto magazine should focus on high-value content.

Part of the inspiration was seeing *Top Gun: Maverick* and how Goose was involved. That summer, I went on a road trip and brainstormed different ideas. The last thing I wrote down in my journal was "Goose." And that's where the idea evolved from because Goose also implied the golden goose. Our goal is to find the next golden goose in crypto. But part of the fable is the farmer killed the goose, hoping to find more golden eggs. So, we will mix in a lot of best practices on how to keep the goose alive and continue earning passive income and growing that golden goose into financial independence.

At the end of 2022, I started putting together the idea. I came up with a mock cover with me on the front and *GOO$E* as the magazine title, and it turned out really well. I showed it to some business leaders within the crypto community, and they said they were in, which was great. I featured them on the cover, which was paid. I got other contributors and some paid advertisers to launch our first magazine in January 2023. It was cool because people saw it and reached out and said, "Hey, we want to help you go big and put you alongside *Bitcoin Magazine* on retail shelves." So, we relaunched in June of 2023 with more content and advertisers, and the journey is just getting started.

Share some key influences or mentors who have played a significant role in your entrepreneurial journey.

Key influencers and mentors have been a big part of my growth. These are key to everyone's growth as we look toward personal development and building our financial wealth.

As I got licensed, I read everything I could that was out there. The first publication I read in 2001 was *Personal Finance for Dummies*. Soon after, I read *Rich Dad, Poor Dad* by Robert Kiyosaki. That book changed my

life. The whole premise of it was the wealthy buy and invest in income-producing assets. Real estate is part of that. He also profiled a couple of other businesses. One of those were dry cleaning businesses, which he said were pretty much recession proof.

In 2006, I also had a mortgage company I was a part of for about four years. I didn't like what I saw in the industry and left that business. My wife at the time and I purchased a dry-cleaning pickup and delivery service. And that was the beginning of income-producing assets. She still owns that business, enjoys the flexibility, and has a decent business going.

Mentorship in crypto was the first thing I looked at besides my research and reading everything I could. I hired someone with a lot more experience than I had, and that ended up going very well for me. It taught me how to properly research the coins and tokens and create criteria and fundamental analyses to help my investing decisions. So, I'm very grateful for that mentorship, and he still mentors me and many of the leaders within that community, which has really grown. That's a valuable asset.

My biggest win from that was turning a $150 investment in 2020 into a $13,000 gain at the beginning of 2021. There are still opportunities like that in crypto, and that is what I want to do for my clients and GOO$E community members. Crypto is just an evolution of the internet. In the dotcom days and along the way in crypto, we saw that huge returns were still available to the average investor. This makes a potentially life-changing opportunity available to all of us who take the time to learn and invest. It doesn't take a lot. Start learning, investing, taking strategic risks, and diversifying so you can be positioned right to take advantage of the next bull run in crypto.

What makes your business unique and valuable?

GOO$E Magazine aims to provide high-value content and education to new and experienced crypto investors. We focus primarily on wealth-minded investors. And this is available to, as I like to say, beginners to ballers in crypto.

There's a lot of what I call the nohelp.com out there in crypto. And we also saw this in the financial world as the internet grew. We had to seek mentors, do research, and read books. We also did not learn any of this from traditional schooling. That is one thing that makes us unique.

As people who strive to be self-reliant and personally responsible, it's with our time and determination that we need to seek out proper information, the right opportunities, and the right risks. We hope to accomplish that with *GOO$E Magazine*, our website, the content we provide, the coursework available to community members, and the group effort of all of us learning together and sharing information.

In this situation, community is key because there is a vast amount of information in cryptocurrency, and not one person can know it all. As we develop more community members who can seek out information to share among the community, we can all do further research and determine if that's something that we want to invest in.

This solves the noise problem in the investment world when it comes to crypto. As we've already seen, there are many pump-and-dumps—meme coins that will skyrocket and then crash because they're not sustainable. There are over 25,000 coins and tokens right now, so there is a lot of noise trying to determine which ones will be the top 100.

Business fundamentals say that 90 percent of all businesses fail within the first five years. In crypto, that can be the first five months. We look for the right investments and create criteria that help us determine if it has a good chance of being around. We think that's a pretty valuable proposition for our community members in helping them navigate the complexity and noise inherent in crypto.

Since we are a media company, we have access to many business leaders and communities to help find innovative founders and emerging companies that have a good chance of being around in the future because we focus on high-value content. We don't publish pump-and-dump schemes just because they want to pay to be in the publication or on our website.

What is one of the most valuable lessons you've learned as an entrepreneur?

Looking back at my entrepreneurial journey, I would say two main lessons come to mind. The first is when it comes to marketing and being seen, I've realized that everything works a little. Unfortunately, this means that we need to market in many ways or through omni channels—platforms that allow our message to get out to the right people (hopefully).

For example, when I ran my financial planning practice, I wrote a book about social security and retirement income strategies called *The Social Security Success Guide*. With that, I ran a successful seminar system that provided leads, further qualified them, and established my credibility to work with my clients. I believe in publishing print and seminar marketing to leverage your expertise in qualified markets. The coolest experience was when a woman called me from Florida to ask for my help after finding my book in a public library.

The second lesson is not to buy into the hype. Cryptocurrency is full of hype. Therefore, discerning all the information and making the right decisions is key. I learned my most valuable lessons back in 2014. Friends and clients came to me in Colorado who wanted to invest in cannabis. And eventually, I found what I thought was a good investment and said, "Me too."

So, we gathered about a half million dollars in this medical marijuana grow. Shortly after, we realized how much professionalism the industry lacked. Everyone bought into the green rush, but it ended up just being a greed rush. We lost a lot of money and dealt with very strict regulations and barriers in banking and marketing that caused us to struggle. We ended up having to close the business.

I took those lessons to *GOO$E Magazine* and my crypto journey. How do we get the word out most effectively? How do we cut through the noise and determine which crypto investments have a good chance of being around in the next five to ten years and into our future? Because ultimately, we're looking for the next Microsoft, Amazon, Google, Apple, or Facebook. I truly believe those are available to investors.

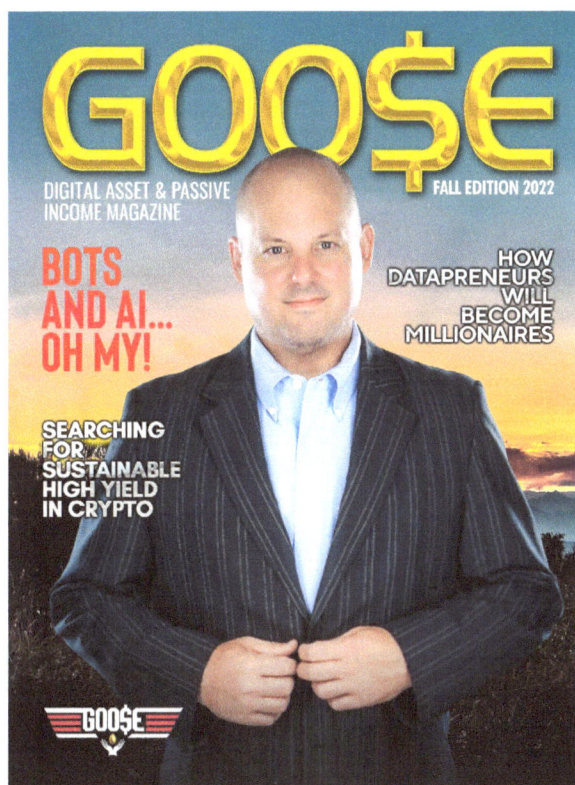

How have you and your business benefited from your involvement with Achieve Systems?

The Achieve community—its valuable resources and experienced team—has played a key part in my success. I was inspired by a guest speaker to launch my own magazine. The Achieve leadership team, Robert and Vanessa Raymond and Michael Libercci, empowered me to think bigger and launch GOO$E into a brand. I'm grateful to do business with many members and form relationships, many of whom I consider friends and family. I highly recommend joining the community, plugging in, and taking action to launch or scale your business.

What does your morning routine look like?

My morning routine has greatly changed due to cryptocurrency being a global industry. When I wake up in the morning, I pray and meditate. Then, I check my email for any fires or newsworthy stories to prepare for the day in case anything important is going on. Next, I exercise, move, or do something active before I get into the busyness of the day. I have my coffee, which I enjoy. Then, I work from home, but I also have an executive office membership that I like for an escape from the distractions of home. There, I can focus on getting work done in a professional setting.

What I need to incorporate into the morning activities is being better at communication and social media. I am planning systems to get information out to our community and prospects who may have an interest in cryptocurrency and building wealth.

What parting words of wisdom do you have for the reader?

My words of wisdom would be: We all need to be better investors. $1 million dollars isn't worth what it used to be. It is so easy to get stuck in the busyness of life and working for an income. I will take some advice from Robert Kiyosaki's Cashflow Quadrant. If you've read *Rich Dad, Poor Dad,* you'll understand, but he talks about ESBI. E is for employee. S is for self-employed. B is for business owner, and I is for investor. The goal is to be a business owner and investor. If you are a Business Owner (B), you can start becoming an Investor (I) by learning how to accept Bitcoin and crypto as payment.

Most of us in our entrepreneurial journey are stuck in S, meaning you own a job. You have no system to continue your legacy if something were to happen, nor do you have a system to continue to generate income while you're not working.

The next goal is to be a business owner, where you're building a team. You have systems that generate income while traveling or enjoying your time off with the family. That is the definition or the purpose of a business.

The final step is to become an investor and pick up investments that pay an income.

While pursuing my crypto journey, I took that same advice into crypto and sought passive income opportunities, finding projects that pay yield. DeFi (decentralized finance) in crypto can be disruptive and is what the banks are concerned about. This may be key in building our portfolios. We help people find projects, companies, and protocols that have a chance to go up tremendously in value. Along the journey, we find opportunities that pay passive income and pay a sustainable yield. This is the ultimate goal. We all have that opportunity. We need to start so we do not get left behind in this last opportunity to have life-changing gains and grow our wealth.

Action Steps

1. Diversify your investment portfolio: After reading the article, you'll understand the importance of diversification, especially in the volatile world of cryptocurrency. Consider spreading your investments across

different types of assets, including crypto, to mitigate risk and increase the potential for returns.

2. Seek mentorship and community: The author emphasizes the value of mentorship and community in making informed investment decisions. Your business can benefit from this by seeking out experts in your industry or joining professional networks to gain insights and share knowledge.

3. Implement omnichannel marketing: The author's experience shows that "everything works a little" when it comes to marketing. To improve your business, consider adopting an omnichannel marketing strategy to reach your target audience through various platforms and mediums, thereby increasing your visibility and potential for customer engagement.

About the Author

Charlie Stivers, a business owner since 2001 with strong family farm values, began his journey from a tech enthusiast who invested in dotcom stocks in 1998 to a professional licensed in 2001. In 2016, he authored the Social Security Success Guide to aid retirees, and in 2020, he embraced cryptocurrencies. Now, he focuses full-time on educating others about blockchain technology and helping people improve their personal economy. His vision is to grow GOO$E into a community-powered publication, emphasizing sustainability and responsible leadership in the decentralized digital asset space.

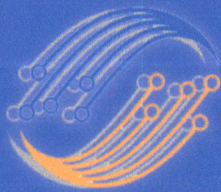

UNLEASHING YOUR POTENTIAL WITH ACHIEVE TV

JULIE ANN MEYER

Chris O'Byrne

Can you choose a story from your childhood you feel was important to becoming who you are today?

Julie Ann Meyer

There are quite a few different options. I don't always like to share this one because it can be a bummer for the people watching and listening. But my mom passed away when I was fourteen. That was life changing. It transformed me on a cellular level. The reason I bring that up is because it could be super painful.

It's been over thirty years, so I think I'm over it by now. And I wouldn't change it because of who I am today, who I became, and what I could do because she passed away. Would

I wish for that to happen? Absolutely not. If I could choose, I wouldn't have chosen that because it was painful at the time, especially as a teenager. However, that was one of those pivotal moments where I saw life differently.

Chris O'Byrne

What lessons did you learn from that? What are some ways your life took a different path?

Julie Ann Meyer

One of the main lessons I learned when I was very young is that life is short. There are no guarantees. Some interesting phenomena happened around my mom's passing away that would be considered supernatural if you're not religious or spiritual. However, seeing those things, I learned that life goes on in a different form. Even though I couldn't experience my mom in her human self, she never left me. She wasn't in my life in a physical form.

Chris O'Byrne

What came in between the age of 14 and starting your first business?

Julie Ann Meyer

I was a baby entrepreneur. I was the kid who went around and asked to wash people's cars. I used to earn money any way I could. I was born into being an entrepreneur. However, I have lived several lifetimes between now and that time.

Some highlights included living in Canada for about six years, where I went to school

and worked in pharmacy. Then, I moved to New York City, where I was a full-time volunteer, bartended, and worked in restaurants. After that, I moved to Italy. I lived there for a while and did window displays for work. It was so much fun. I had so many wonderful experiences.

Those are also examples of things I wouldn't have been able to do had my mom not passed away. She left me some money, making it easier for me to have these experiences at a younger age. Those experiences changed me as well.

Eventually, I moved back to New York and then California, where I worked in addiction recovery. That can suck your soul out if you let it. There is so much trauma, drama, and heaviness that I needed to move forward with helping people in their wellness journey.

I decided to work for myself and become a personal trainer and nutrition coach. That was my first real experience as an adult, entirely on my own, for myself, working in that industry. But it turned into a TV show and now my TV network. It's been interesting because it's not necessarily a path I would have chosen, but who I was created opportunities for opportunities and experiences to fall into my lap.

Chris O'Byrne

What is your current business, and what inspired you to start it?

Julie Ann Meyer

I love this question because it's my baby. I run *Achieve TV*, and we are a vision distribution network. It came about because I had my TV show and started training people how to do what I do. I was offered a TV network, which was pretty amazing. I started it from the ground up. It's been highly successful because I wanted to create a place where people with a message, hope, and lessons to share can get those out on a larger platform. I provide that for them.

I want to empower people to not die with their music inside of them. If I can be the irrigation system, and they're the little sprinkler sprouts, they can sprinkle out their knowledge and entertainment for more people than I could on my own. That's the idea behind it. It's inspirational and hopeful and a place for entrepreneurs to find answers and community.

Chris O'Byrne

If I'm hearing you correctly, what drives you is the opportunity to help entrepreneurs

and business leaders achieve their dreams by getting their vision out. Entrepreneurs are all about making a vision become reality. Because it's so powerful, you're helping them reach more people and increase their influence through this media.

Julie Ann Meyer

That's correct. My main goal has always been to help people. This is a better way for me to leave a positive legacy for many people because I love helping people achieve what they want and dream of, especially the ones trying to help others. I hope to make it easier and streamline a process for them so they can create influence they might not otherwise have. They can be seen.

I often think about this for musicians. How many fabulous musicians and singers are out there that never make it big? My platform is for people who don't have an opportunity to shine the way they should. There are so many talented people who deserve to be seen and heard.

Chris O'Byrne

Who are some of the key influences or mentors you've had?

Julie Ann Meyer

I've been blessed. It's true that when the student is ready, the teacher appears. My first coach was a previous Zen monk. He spent fourteen years in a monastery. His name is Alex Mill. I randomly ran across one of his books at Barnes and Noble and picked it up. It was an impulse buy, and it changed my life. When I reached out to him, I wasn't expecting him to pick me as a student, but he did. That changed the trajectory of my life. That was the major one because everything stemmed from that.

Another important experience was going to the taping of World's Greatest Motivators.

Bob Proctor, Mary Morrissey, Les Brown, John Assaraff, Lisa Nichols, Jack Canfield, and many others were there—so many greats. It also changed the trajectory of where I was going and opened my eyes to what's possible.

Brian Tracy was also there, and I will be in a book with him next year. Going from seeing people on stage to being included in that group in such a short time—not even three years—is pretty amazing.

Another more recent influence is Robert Raymond. He is the CEO of Achieve Systems. He's been a guiding force in my life and a good friend. He and his wife, Vanessa, even came to my wedding. Those are the three most pivotal people and experiences that have changed me.

Chris O'Byrne

How do you manage to get into a book with Brian Tracy?

Julie Ann Meyer

It all started with my TV show. When I say it can open doors, it honestly can. I interviewed on a red carpet on New Year's Eve and met the CEO of the LA Tribune. He and I became business partners and affiliates, and he offered me a position in the female thought leader special edition of the LA Tribune. That will be turned into a chapter and is how I ended up with Brian Tracy.

Chris O'Byrne

I love how that flows from one incredible experience to the next.

Julie Ann Meyer

It's been amazing. You never know what will happen if you are open to the possibilities. I've been guilty of being focused on how I will get somewhere versus allowing whatever shows up to be the way. I've missed a lot of opportunities. I still have my eye on the prize of where I want to go, but when I became more open to how, so many more things have shown up in my life. Now, I can dream bigger, and more things have happened.

My business partner said something fascinating. He said we'll have a business plan to get from A to B, but people don't realize that you take left turns, right turns, and about-faces; it's never A to B. Never. You don't know, but it's still the path. It's still the way you will get there. It does not look how you expect it because you don't know what's coming. You might have to take a right turn to get to your point B. Even though it doesn't seem like a straight line, it is because that's the way you have to go.

Chris O'Byrne

Can you share how you met Rob Raymond from Achieve Systems?

Julie Ann Meyer

Yes, that was through my TV show as well. I had on a lovely gentleman named Ari Gronich. He said, "You have to meet this guy, Robert Raymond. He's so amazing. He's going to change your life." I thought, *Yeah, whatever. I don't think so.*

Rob reached out to me through Facebook, and he was never pushy, which I liked. He asked to meet with me, and I didn't respond. Then, I discovered he lived on the same block as me. His second home in California was on the same block as mine, only a five-minute walk away. I thought that was too coincidental, so I decided I should meet him.

The funny part is that the day I met him, it was raining so hard; it was raining cats and dogs! I had about forty-five minutes in between my client and meeting him. I thought about canceling because of how bad the rain was, but I didn't. I met him, and it was one of the best choices I've ever made because he really did change my life.

Chris O'Byrne

How has Achieve changed your life?

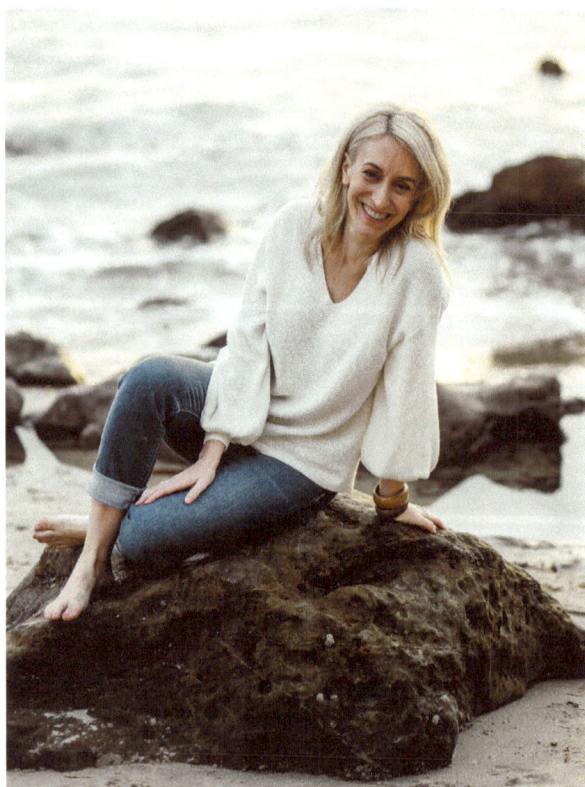

Julie Ann Meyer

Rob has taught me to think bigger than I thought possible. Achieve offers many incredible things. My favorite parts are the conferences three to four times a year. Those have evolved as well. Between my first and third one, I've met many more people, which makes it fun. It was like seeing old friends, but I've also gotten a lot of business through doing that. I've grown a lot, too.

I've authored another book. The TV program about how to teach people how to do what I do was Rob's idea. I was planning to sell my show to radio. Overall, Achieve is a place to grow and build dreams. Whatever you want to achieve, they offer something to help you get where you want to go. There are plenty of mentors. There are plenty of people who you can connect with to grow your business. Plus, there's a lot of education. If you are missing something, you'll likely find it there.

It's very individualized because I started with this coaching idea of how everything would look, but you know how it is. Launch and adjust.

While there is a basic formula to make a show profitable and, more importantly, influential, I bring out the genius in each person so they can showcase that and attract the right people to their show. You won't attract the right people if you're not authentically presenting yourself. The focus is: How will the show look? What information will you give? How will it be entertaining? And what tips and tricks will you use to grow your audience quickly? Because certain things work for certain people, and there are others they'll never do because they don't like doing them. I could tell you to do something, but it won't be helpful if you don't do it. I figure out ways to make people utilize their skills and grow their show. It's enjoyable. It's not that hard. It doesn't take that long.

We also have a lot of continuing education and masterminds, so people aren't left alone as they grow. Achieve is a community. It gives people a place to go and share what is working, what isn't, and what they've tried. Everyone helps each other.

Chris O'Byrne

I recently signed for your coaching. We haven't even had our first session yet, but just thinking about doing my TV show has got me thinking about how I present myself in casual conversations, on Zoom videos, and on social media. It has changed my idea of how people are perceiving me. What image am I putting forth? Is it an image I'm proud of or that my family would be proud of?

When I was younger, I would try to be the funny guy. I did and said things I wasn't proud of. But now I think, *How do I help people in every conversation?* Instead of trying to present myself in a positive light, I focus on the other person and try to build them up.

Julie Ann Meyer

It's fascinating that you say that, because the thing that most people don't realize, whether or not they have a TV show, is there's always somebody watching. Always. We don't know it because not everybody tells us they're watching.

Once, I was walking from the gym to my car, and this woman ran out of a nearby restaurant and said, "Excuse me." The New Yorker in me was ready to pretend I didn't see or hear her. But I'm glad I stopped because she said, "I see you walking from the gym pretty much every day, and I wanted to tell you how inspirational you are to me." She worked at the restaurant, and she'd seen my body change. She said, "I'm just so inspired by you." There I was, just walking to my car. I had no idea. I'd never seen her before. I haven't seen her since, and I never would have known had she not come out to tell me. I was just living my life. Everyone has somebody like that. I'm not special in that respect.

Chris O'Byrne

What's a valuable lesson you've learned along the way?

Julie Ann Meyer

The main lesson is that allowing yourself to be seen can be scary. It's a very vulnerable experience. However, to have the most positive impact on other people, you have to allow yourself to be seen. It's scary.

I'm pretty introverted, and I like my alone time and am not comfortable being out there, as they say. But I know that if I don't show up and share things that may be embarrassing, the things that I've done, or things I'm not necessarily proud of, I'm not letting other people know what's possible. If they are in the spot where I was before, they don't have to let those things define who they are. It doesn't matter what you did. It only matters who you are now.

Chris O'Byrne

I'm curious, what does your morning routine look like?

Julie Ann Meyer

The first thing I do is take care of my fur babies. They are the number one priority. But even before that, I thank God for the unexpected miracles and blessings coming my way that day. Then, I write down three things I'm grateful for, which must be different daily. That way, I can expand the goodness around me and see what's positive. I always drink water, and I try to get some exercise in.

The last thing I do is "thinkitate." I can't remember who coined that term, but it's called thinkitate instead of meditate. I'll think about an idea I have, or I'll brainstorm. Or I'll think about how I want to show up that day. What do I want to accomplish? I set those intentions during that time.

The important thing about setting intentions that many people don't consider is checking in. Did you do it? Because we can set all the intentions in the world, but if we don't follow through, our intentions don't mean much. It took me an embarrassingly long time to figure that out.

I like my mornings to be fun. I get a lot more work done in the early morning and mid-afternoon. It just depends on the day. But there are certain times of the day when I'm the most productive, so I try to honor that.

Chris O'Byrne

One thing I like to do when I remember is a list of ten, which I learned from James Altucher. It doesn't matter what that list is, but once you get into it, you start coming up with a lot of ideas. For example, I might ask, what are ten new services I could offer in my business? What are ten new columns I could have in my magazine? It doesn't have to be business related; it could be anything. Those first five or six come easily. It's fun because it's creative and jump-starts your creativity. However, those last few can be the toughest. Sometimes, you end up with a huge list. Sometimes, it's a struggle to come up with ten. Like thinkitating, it forces you to focus, think more deeply and creatively, and pull inspiration from other sources.

Julie, what parting wisdom would you like to leave us with?

Julie Ann Meyer

My parting wisdom is that you are enough just as you are. You have lived a worthy life if you can help just one person daily. Most people don't realize they are enough as they are. They're trying to do and be things versus just showing up. Being who we are will make the most significant impact and create the most extraordinary influence—not only for ourselves but for the people around us.

Action Steps

1. Reevaluate your business vision: Inspired by the author's journey with Achieve TV, take some time to revisit and possibly redefine the vision for your own business. Make sure it aligns with your core values and long-term goals. This will help you stay focused and attract the right opportunities and partnerships.

2. Invest in personal branding: The author emphasized the importance of allowing yourself to be seen and heard. Consider investing in personal branding efforts that showcase your unique skills and values. This could be through social media, a blog, or even starting your own podcast or video series. By doing so, you'll not only improve your business's visibility but also build a more authentic connection with your audience.

3. Implement a mentorship program: The author's success was partly due to the guidance received from key mentors. To accelerate your own business growth, seek out mentors who can provide valuable insights and advice. Alternatively, offer mentorship to others in your industry or team. This reciprocal relationship can lead to new perspectives, increased motivation, and a stronger network, all of which can significantly benefit your business.

About the Author

Julie Ann Meyer is the president of Achieve TV, a Vision Distribution Network. Her mission is to help as many entrepreneurs as possible to shine brightly and share their messages on a grand scale. Learn more at ownyourwellness.net.

JOIN
Achieve Systems

BECOME AN ACHIEVE SYSTEMS MEMBER TODAY!

Education

We help you get the tools to create a thriving business! It's turnkey, you can start NOW!

Marketing

We provide marketing guidelines but also plug you into our conferences, events and database

Community

We have a thriving community of entrepreneurs and business owners for you to collaborate, refer and partner with to grow and up-level your business!

WE WORK WITH ENTREPRENEURS, BUSINESS OWNERS, SPEAKERS & LEADERS!

CONTACT US OR REGISTER HERE: www.AchieveSystemsPro.com

THE 70-20-10 RULE: A GAME-CHANGER IN BUSINESS AND LIFE

WENDY WATSON

Chris O'Byrne:

Going back to childhood, is there a story you can share that was important in helping you become who you are today?

Wendy Watson:

There's not one story in particular, but one of the biggest things was going to work for my parents. I started working for my parents at eleven. My dad was a contractor, so I would go to the construction site with a bunch of grown men. As the contractor's daughter and a female on a construction site, there was a lot of assertiveness.

On the other weekends, I would go to work with my mom in an office with a bunch of women. The two worlds didn't mix, that's for sure. For me, it was confusing, trying to bounce back and forth. But the benefit is I got to see both sides. I learned how to assert myself as the boss's daughter on the construction site with a bunch of grown men. I also got the environment of the softer office political environment. I'm very much like a dualist. I was able to develop both sides of my brain so I could learn how to work in both.

Chris O'Byrne:

Was there any one of those in particular that you felt more comfortable with?

Wendy Watson:

I feel more comfortable on the construction site than I do in an office, which is why I don't work in an office anymore.

Chris O'Byrne:

Why do you think that is?

Wendy Watson:

I don't deal with politics very well. I don't play games. I'm a truth speaker. I'm a truth seeker. That is not usually the case in an office. You have to beat around the bush and play nice with the boss, and all those politics-type things feel fake to me. I don't do well in those environments. Being an entrepreneur, owning my space, speaking my message, and being around like-minded people is more my environment.

Chris O'Byrne:

What came between graduating high school and starting your business?

Wendy Watson:

I had a lot of losing jobs because I was too abrasive. That also came into play in my first marriage, divorce, and second marriage. That time also included two bankruptcies and a lot of chaos and toxicity.

Chris O'Byrne:

How did you grow out of that?

Wendy Watson:

When working for corporate America and dating my second ex-husband, my audit manager gave me the 70-20-10 rule. Growing up on a construction site with an entrepreneur, you have to find a way to say yes to the client and make the client happy. There's no ifs, ands, or buts about it. You have to think outside the box. You have to do whatever it takes. That created a perfectionist mentality, which doesn't do well in an office.

While I was great at my job and good with numbers, it did not bode well for creating healthy working relationships with my coworkers, inner departments, and other bosses. I would get bypassed for promotions because I wasn't working well with others.

My audit manager gave me the 70-20-10 rule. He explained the goal was for 70 percent of the invoices to go through without incident, for only 20 percent to get escalated to management, and to write off 10 percent. I couldn't believe they'd be willing to write stuff off. That was a new concept

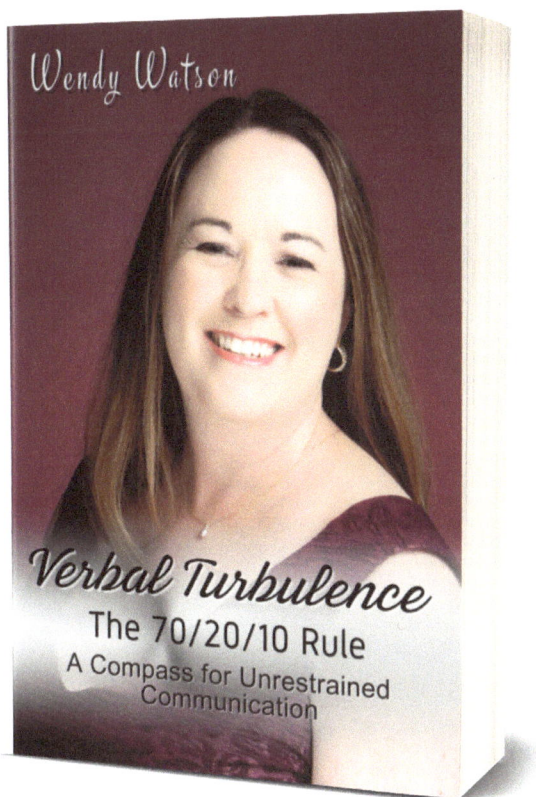

for me. I had to process it. Then I realized I didn't have to be perfect.

I think that's essential for entrepreneurs, athletes, and women to realize. Many women think we have to be Superwoman—go to work, get the kids ready, make dinner, pay the bills, and do all these things—before we can even relax. If we don't get that stuff done, we punish ourselves.

I took that 70-20-10 rule and looked at it through the lens of communication. That was a life-changer for me because my biggest struggle was communication. What is the 70 percent that people are projecting at me? What is the 20 percent? What is the 10 percent? How much of a conversation is useful to me? Are they projecting their baggage, fears, memories, and emotions? How

much of that are they projecting, and how much of that is useful to me so I don't take on somebody else's emotions, beliefs, and baggage and then flip it around? What am I doing to other people?

There's a lot of self-reflection. Active listening is the biggest thing. Actively listen, not just to others, but to yourself. What are you saying to yourself? If you're not willing to say it to your mother, why are you saying it to yourself? We are our worst critics.

Why are we being so hard on ourselves? Let's find 10 percent of grace. And being like, "Out of all the lists I had, how much did I get done versus how much I didn't? Out of the big, long list I had to do today as an entrepreneur, how much of that did I get done?" Then, when you go to bed, you're not punishing yourself for everything you didn't get done on your to-do list. It's okay to not get things done. Maybe some things get done tomorrow. Maybe things will get done next week. And then end with gratitude, realizing all you did get done.

Chris O'Byrne:

How long ago did you start your business?

Wendy Watson:

I started my massage business in 2014. During the recession in 2009, working for corporate America, I got restructured. I got caught up in all the restructuring. It felt suffocating to go back to a cubicle. When I got let go, I was in a lead position, a middle position. During the recession, they were getting rid of all the middle positions.

I was overqualified to be a clerk; I was under-qualified to be a manager, so I wasn't getting hired anyway. I made a list of everything I wanted my new career to have. I knew I couldn't afford a four-year degree, nor did I have the time. I looked at vocational options, and massage therapy checked all the boxes. I checked out a school on Friday, and everything felt right. Everything felt synchronistic. It felt like it was in harmony with what I was looking for. The class started on Monday, or I had to wait another month. My entrepreneurial decision-making told me to go for it, so I signed all the paperwork, and I started class on Monday.

Chris O'Byrne:

You started as a massage therapist. How did that progress to what you're offering now?

Wendy Watson:

As a massage therapist, I work on peoples' bodies and energies. I gravitated toward the energy and modalities—reflexology, polarity, cranial sacral, and acupressure. As I was learning and practicing those on my clients, I noticed how much more profound an effect it had on them. It's not just rubbing their lower back muscles because their back hurts but taking it a step further to find the root of the problem instead of just addressing the pain issue.

The more I learned about that, the more I applied it to my life. After my second divorce and loss of a child, I went through my healing phase and asked myself, *Why am I attracting these people? What am I doing to surround myself with these narcissistic,* *addictive personalities, the partygoers with all these toxic behaviors? What am I doing?*

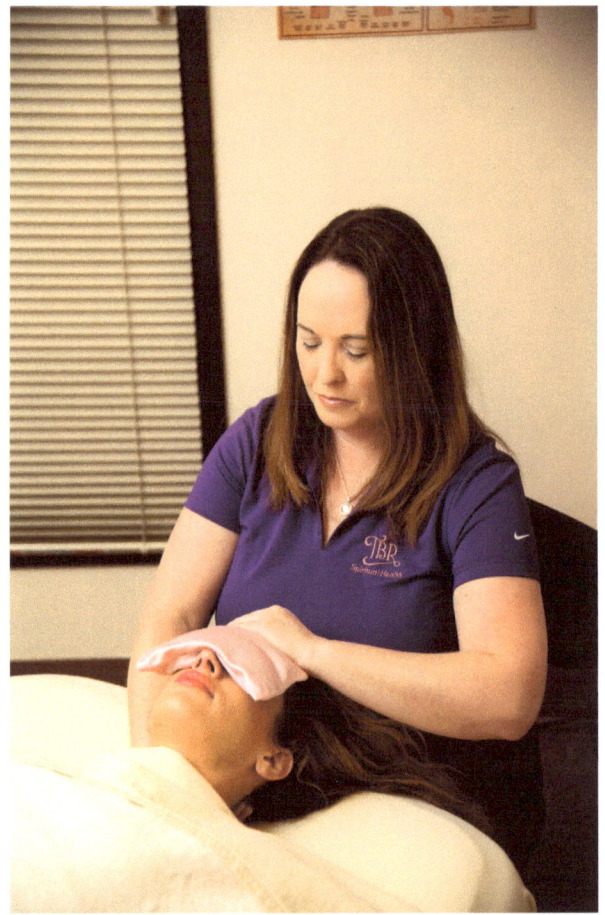

I focused on self-healing and a lot of inner reflection, looking at my agreements, contracts, and habits. I think for most people, it all comes down to their habits. What did we learn from our parents? What did we learn from friends? And do they work for us?

As I was going through all that and learning, I was also life-coaching for my clients. And that's when I learned how valuable it was for them to save their marriages. One client contributes the last seven years of her marriage to my coaching. I've helped somebody escape suicidal tendencies and find a new perspective on life, a new path, and a new journey. Seeing how profound that is for other people, I knew I was meant to do that on a greater scale, not just one-on-one and one at a time.

My massage business progressed to the point where I reached my ceiling as a solo practitioner. At that point, 95 percent or higher of my clients were veterans. I wasn't getting any new clients, so I wasn't getting any fresh money. My cash flow was getting stagnant.

The only way I could grow would be to go full-scale and open a studio, hire people, and go through that whole rigmarole, which I didn't want to do. I didn't want to babysit employees. I didn't want to be in Uncle Sam's pocket. I didn't want to be on that radar. I decided to close my business, move to Denver, and rebrand. I wanted to help people cultivate their inner relationships, get down to the root of the issues, and create harmony in their lives so that they don't have this ripple effect of negativity. I wanted to do this on a much larger scale.

Chris O'Byrne:

How are you doing it on a larger scale?

Wendy Watson:

First, I wrote my book, *Verbal Turbulence: The 70/20/10 Rule*, which was recently published.

Second, I will be doing speaking engagements. I'm regularly on podcasts and TV shows. And I joined Achieve, which gives me a larger audience.

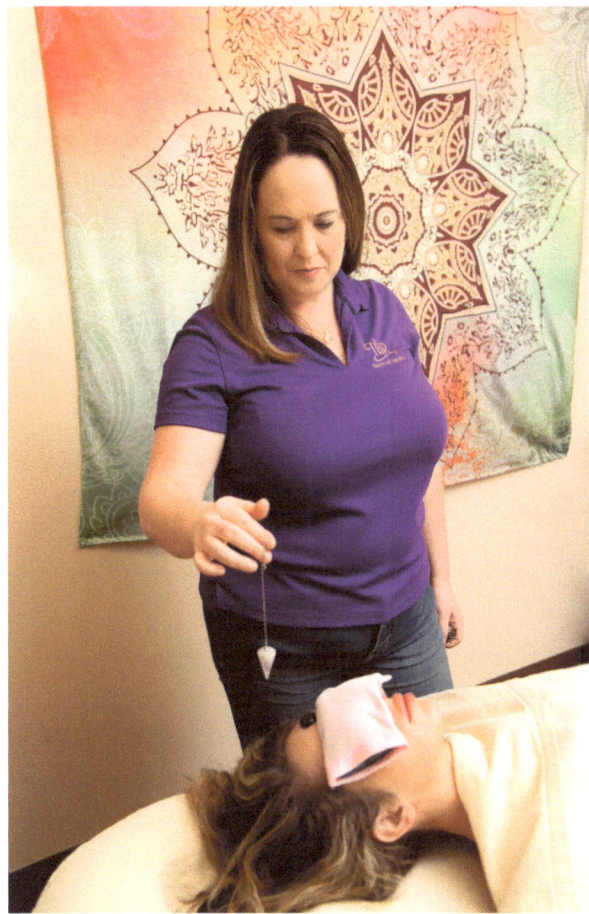

Chris O'Byrne:

What makes what you do unique?

Wendy Watson:

Many people tell me, "I had this little voice in my head tell me I should take a different route to work. But I didn't know what it was or where it came from, so I just took my normal route to work. Then, there ended up being a car accident, and I was late for a meeting or late for work," or whatever it was.

I help them learn how to listen to and trust their inner voice. It's just like in business. We have to learn to know, like, and trust.

So, how do we get you to know, like, and trust your inner voice, intuition, and spirit? As Neanderthals, that was all that we had. Now, we have all this technology and all these things that get in the way of us listening to ourselves and making decisions that are in alignment with ourselves. How do we get back to that?

Chris O'Byrne:

What are some of the biggest problems you help your clients with?

Wendy Watson:

Cultivating healthy relationships and overcoming trauma. Those are the top issues that humans have. Most people don't know how to cultivate healthy relationships. And it all starts with ourselves. Our most important relationship is our relationship with ourselves.

If we're unhappy with ourselves, we project that into the rest of our relationships, whether in business, family, or romantic. If we negatively talk to ourselves—if we're body shaming or punishing ourselves because we didn't get our task list done—we do the same thing with everybody else. And that doesn't cultivate natural, healthy relationships where we can help support each other to be the best version of ourselves.

Chris O'Byrne:

You said earlier that you went through some self-analysis and improvement and figured out some things relating to your relationships and how you attract certain people. What were some of the biggest changes you made to change who you were attracting in your life?

Wendy Watson:

One of the biggest ahas was that it reflected my childhood and my family. We think what we grow up with is normal. If you grow up poor, you don't know what to do with money if you get it. You think not having money is normal. Being poor is normal. When you're surrounded by addiction, drugs, and emotional immaturity, you think that is normal. You don't think there's anything wrong with it. Those are the people you end up attracting. That was a big aha.

Additionally, I saw some habits I picked up from my family, like suppressing my emotions. I'm a truth speaker. However, because I was raised in an environment with a lot of fighting, I didn't want to instigate fighting or fight too much. While I would voice my opinion, I wouldn't push it past a certain point because I wanted to avoid arguing. While dealing with somebody who's also volatile or emotionally and verbally abusive, there's only so far you can push it. Then, you start suppressing or, as I did, suppress emotions. Eventually, that explodes into a much bigger argument. I also learned ways to communicate so it was more easily digestible.

Chris O'Byrne:

What would you say has been one of the most valuable lessons you've learned as an entrepreneur?

Wendy Watson:

The 70-20-10 rule is the biggest thing because I can use it in communication. I can use it in my business metrics. I used it in my massage career.

When I started as a massage therapist, I worked for a corporate franchise. I was in a new industry. I went from accounting to massage. I was in an entirely different world. I didn't know how that world worked. I knew the best way to learn was to start at the ground level, work my way up, and build my resume to learn the industry.

At the first job I had, they told me that their goal for their client retention rate was 35 percent. I said, "If that were a test, that's failing!" I didn't understand why an F was a goal.

I determined that when I went and worked out on my own and started my own business, I wanted a 70 percent retention rate. I wanted 70 percent of my clients to be happy, regular, and satisfied clients. Twenty percent could be the irregular ones who came in less frequently, and then the 10 percent would be the new clients or the ones who only came in once every five years.

Setting that goal—a much higher goal—was very fruitful. That's how I built my business to the point where I reached my ceiling and had to decide what direction I wanted to go.

During the last six years I was in Phoenix with my massage business, I had a 68 percent retention rate over a three-month period and a six-month period. When I present it to other people as far as employee retention rates, wouldn't you want to have 70 percent of your employees happy, productive, efficient employees? Around 20 percent might need improvement or to be under an improvement plan, and 10 percent would be your new hires and fires. Wouldn't that be ideal? That way, you don't have as much employee turnover. You're not spending money on training. You're not spending money on going out and hiring and recruiting. You could save many wasted resources.

Chris O'Byrne:

How has Achieve helped you?

Wendy Watson:

They have given me all the resources I could need, and not just the resources, but the guidance. I just rebranded in January of this year, eight months ago. They mentored me on how to write my book. They helped me self-publish. They helped me launch my book. And not only that. Last year, I was like a snake shedding its skin—new environment, new household, new state, new friends, new everything.

Now, I'm on this new journey of rebranding: What do I want that to look like? How do I create my message? How do I do all of these things? I don't even know people out here, so how do I find the resources I need to build this business?

As a massage therapist, I didn't need to market. I had a 68 percent retention rate for six years and never paid for marketing. I didn't have to do any of that stuff. Now, nobody knows me out here. With Achieve's mentorship and masterminds, as long as you show up, everything works. They've shown me a different level of business and people to surround myself with to up-level myself so that I can up-level the business.

Chris O'Byrne:

You are now one of the Achieve alpha leaders. What does that mean?

Wendy Watson:

To me, that means respect and honor. They see that I have great leadership skills, helping others build themselves up, and self-leadership, which I think is even more important because you need to lead by example. The respect and the honor that they see in me is the biggest thing for me.

To become an alpha leader, you have to be a leader. You must lead yourself to make decisions, follow through, be in alignment with yourself, and be a go-getter. You can't just sit around twiddling your thumbs, waiting for the book to get written. You have to sit down and write the book. I think that has a lot to do with it, but also caring about other people, wanting the best for other people, and wanting to help uplift your fellow people.

Chris O'Byrne:

What parting words of wisdom or advice would you like to give?

Wendy Watson:

I just posted this on social media yesterday: Do you make decisions out of habit, emotions, logic, or intentions? By operating through intention, you are analyzing the habits and finding a balance between the emotions and logic. And you're taking all of those to find the right direction. Going through the thinking and emotional processes and fine-tuning that intention you want.

When we operate out of habits, we're not thinking. We're not making sure that's what we want to do or is in alignment with ourselves. When you're too far into the emotions, you're only making emotional decisions, so you're not collecting data and going through the logical aspects. When you're only going through the logic, then you don't know how you feel about the decision that you're making because you're only using data. By being intentional, you go through the habits, emotions, and logic and devise a clear and concise intention.

Action Steps

1. **Implement the 70-20-10 rule:** After reading the author's insights, consider applying the 70-20-10 rule to various aspects of your business, such as customer or employee retention. Aim for 70% of interactions to go smoothly, allow 20% to require some management intervention, and be prepared to write off 10%. This approach can help you set more realistic goals and reduce stress.

2. **Focus on active listening:** The author emphasized the importance of active listening not just to others but also to yourself. Take time to actively listen to your employees, customers, and even your own inner dialogue. This can improve your decision-making, team dynamics, and customer relations, ultimately benefiting your business.

3. **Be intentional in decision-making:** The author advises making decisions based on a balance of habit, emotion, and logic. Start by analyzing your current decision-making processes. Are they mostly emotional, logical, or habitual? Strive for a balanced, intentional approach that considers all three aspects. This can lead to more aligned and effective business choices.

About the Author

Wendy Watson is a spiritual therapist who helps others cultivate healthy inner relationships that extend outward. She has spent the past twenty years transforming herself several times over and developing her five pillars: self-leadership, self-awareness, self-ownership, effective communication, and trailblazing skills. Wendy is excited to help you on your journey using such skills as her 70/20/10 Rule.

Cultivating Healthy Business Relationships

Wendy Watson
Verbal Turbulence
The 70/20/10 Rule
A Compass for Unrestrained Communication

Wendy's book is available on Amazon

"You can't build trust and loyalty without effective communication"

Workshops include:

Self-Ownership

Self-Leadership

Self-Awareness

Trailblazing Skillset

Effective Communication

For more Information
Wendy@TBRSpiritualhealth.com
www.TBRSpiritualHealth.com

Call Wendy
602.689.1695

OWNING YOUR WORTH IN THE MARKETPLACE

LILA VERONICA

Choose a story from your childhood that you feel was important in becoming who you are today.

One story from childhood that was instrumental in developing me into who I am today is that I used to sell Blow Pops in middle school. My older brother and I would ride our bicycles to the local grocery store called Meijer, which is in the Midwest and one of the first supercenter stores. They had bulk candy. I recognized I could buy Blow Pops for about four to six cents apiece and then sell them at school for twenty-five cents apiece.

I became well-known as somebody you could go to for candy in middle school. One day, my math teacher stood in front of the class and said to everybody, "Now, I'm not going to point out anybody specifically, but I'm going to let you know that selling things in school is not allowed." I quickly realized that I'd get in trouble if I didn't stop selling

Blow Pops in school. However, I was grateful for my math teacher because she allowed me to choose to stop the activity that would get me in trouble instead of just letting me get in trouble.

I learned that it's often better to ask for forgiveness than permission. I didn't even have to ask for forgiveness; it was gifted to me by my teacher, addressing the entire classroom. The other lesson I learned was that I could create money for myself; I could earn money. Maybe I wasn't doing it in a way that would work long-term by selling Blow Pops, but I could get creative and earn money.

As a result, I began washing my parents' friends' cars when they'd come over. I'd immediately approach them and ask if I could wash their car. I charged $10 for a car wash and $20 for a wash and wax. For a kid, $20 went pretty far. I wanted money mostly just to enjoy life. I wanted to be able to buy food, candy, clothes, and the things a normal young woman likes.

In high school, I bought a nail kit, and at homecoming and prom and between different activities, I invited girls to my house or went to their houses to do their nails. I invested in an acrylic nail set and charged them $15, less than they could get their nails done at a salon.

Early on, I recognized that I could create wealth by getting creative, and I've been able to do that repeatedly throughout my adult life. Even when I had a job, I usually had what they now call a side hustle or a side gig, where I would share the things I love and get a commission for them. When eBay came out, I went to thrift stores and bought clothes to sell on eBay. I once bought a Nanette Lepore dress for $4. I knew brand names because I looked at *In Style* magazine all the time. I sold it for $400 on eBay. Those Blow Pops in middle school inspired me to create more and more wealth for myself for years to come.

What inspired you to start your business?

I never thought I would be a business owner. I was a lifelong student and an academic. I taught environmental policy at The Ohio State University and faced a challenging time in my life. As my younger brother likes to say, I had an, "Eat, Pray, Love," moment. I got into yoga and attended a workshop in Long Island, New York. For the first time in my life, I physically felt love for myself, and I chased it.

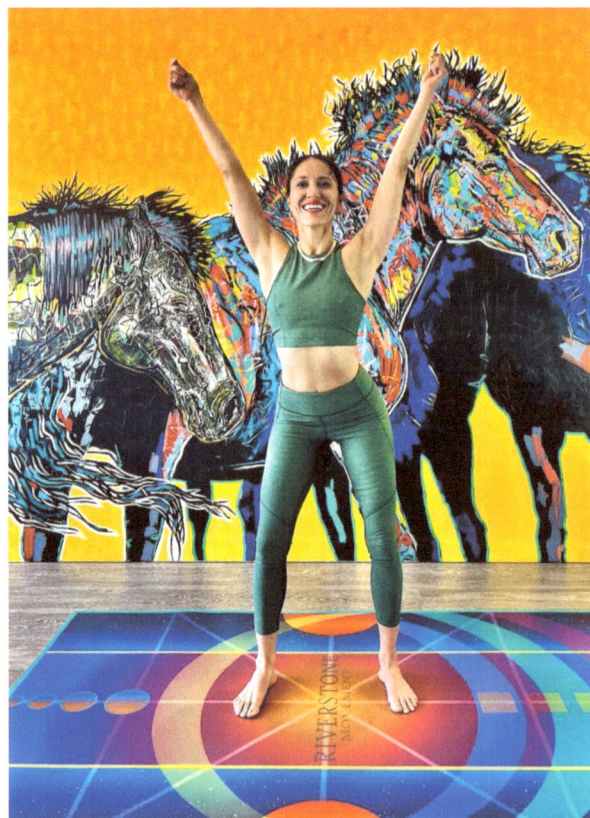

I left my academic career, moved across the country to Colorado, and started learning, practicing, training, and teaching a mindful movement system that transformed how I thought and felt about myself. I learned how I was connected to everything.

During that process, a friend introduced me to the idea of creating six-figures in my life. I had never imagined making a six-figure income, because I'd always been a person who just wanted to help people. I didn't care about the money. I just wanted to save the environment and help people love and feel good about themselves. However, my friend introduced me to the idea of creating six-figures for myself by writing the steps down on a yellow piece of paper, showing me exactly what it would take to create six-figures. I thought to myself, "*I'm doing it! If someone else can do it, I can, too!*"

I started going to business workshops and networking events, learning how to package, price, sell, and market offers. I got introduced to the idea of coaching one day and joined my first coaching program. I went through three coaching programs with that coach and still didn't earn six-figures. It didn't take long to recognize that I needed somebody to help me. I couldn't be in a group program and figure it out. I needed somebody to help me independently, so I hired a private coach. *That* was when I was able to create over six-figures—and I've been able to create more than six-figures for years since.

By going to the workshops, training, receiving coaching, and hiring a private coach, I helped more people at a greater level by earning more money. I learned that money was just my spirit's energy in action in the marketplace. What I know now is that years ago, when I physically felt love for myself and decided to chase that, doing so allowed me to help clients worldwide.

I've worked with people on all seven continents and helped them earn money, feel good in their bodies, and love themselves more. I learned that your net worth is related to your self-worth. If I could look back and do anything differently, I wouldn't because the transformation from loving myself and earning money has been such a beautiful journey that I get to share with so many people worldwide.

Share some key influences or mentors who have played a significant role in your entrepreneurial journey.

The first person I would like to thank is Kris Ward, who had a coaching program called Abundant Yogi, where she coached hundreds of people over the years. Whether you were a yoga teacher, healer, or coach, she showed you how to create wealth and have the mindset you need to have a successful business. She taught me accountability and how to let go of victim mentality and step into an empowered mentality.

The second mentor I'd like to thank is Linda Caducoy. Linda is my former private business coach, now my financial investment mentor—and the person who believed in me when I wasn't sure if I could create six-figures in my business. She saw something in me and let me know that I could earn as much money as I wanted, helping as many people as possible. Linda Caducoy has helped me see my worth, value myself in the marketplace, and has shown me unconditional love with zero judgment.

I'd also like to thank Robert and Vanessa Raymond, who are the leaders of Achieve, as they have allowed me to be seen and heard and share my gifts with their community. One thing that I really love about Robert and Vanessa is that they are truly loving souls who are heartfelt business leaders and love lifting up other people. They taught me that

you can be loving, a helper in the world, and earn a lot of money. They've impacted my business so much because they've helped me open my mind to new ideas. I've been able to invent a Mindful Movement custom mat for my students. They've opened my mind to bigger speaking opportunities and brought my business ideas to a whole new level, while staying healthy. They've shown me new partners and stressed the importance of collaboration and referrals. They make me feel like I don't have to do business

alone and remind me I'm supported and loved. And they've also shown me that it's okay to lean on people in difficult times.

I'd also like to thank the late, but great Louise Hay, who has written many books. My favorite book is called, *You Can Heal Your Life*, because it explains the thought patterns associated with the manifestations in your body. So, whatever is going on in your body is going on in your thoughts. For example, lower back pain is associated with worries about money, safety, and security on Planet Earth. I've been able to use this book to coach my clients all around the world to look at what's going on with their bodies and how it is directly related to their businesses, relationships, and every aspect of their lives. It's also helped me show my clients how to change their thought patterns.

What makes your business unique and valuable?

My business offerings are unique and extremely valuable to all my customers and clients worldwide because they specifically address their self-worth. I have an umbrella that I talk about that covers all my services (the umbrella is owning your worth), and I do this in three unique ways.

The first way is I help my clients own their worth is through embodiment practices, feeling the feelings of their self-worth, vision, and body, and positioning their body in a form that dictates the function of high self-worth. Mindful movement is all about bringing your mind into your body and moving from your entire body. When my clients learn how to live from their entire selves and spend time with their entire selves—minds, bodies, and energies—they value themselves more. When they spend time with themselves and value themselves more, other people value them more.

The second piece of owning your worth is charging what you're worth. In addition to embodiment practices and mindful movement, I help my clients who are business owners in the service-based world to create, package, price, sell, and market high-value offers to high-value clients. I like to call these high-value offers because high-value clients who are grateful want something of high value. They don't want something cheap. And what's neat about selling high-value offers is that you get to receive and earn wealth at a high level. You get to add a lot of value to the marketplace as well. When you add more value to the market and receive more wealth for the value you add to the market, your self-worth increases. When your self-worth increases, your body is healthier. You stand in a new way. And so, embodiment practices and mindful movement are directly related to your wealth creation, which is directly related to your embodiment. Your health and wealth are directly related.

These are the kinds of services that I can offer my clients that are unique. I'm one of the only coaches in the industry who can show you how to create wealth and stay healthy, while not burning out. I'm not about the hustle game. I'm about the alignment game. When you're in alignment in your body, and you're in alignment in receiving wealth for the value that you're offering the world, you're extremely healthy, have great energy, and people love to connect with you.

The third and final piece of owning your worth is I help my clients invest in themselves. I see a lot of entrepreneurs create a lot of wealth, and then they don't know what to do with their money. So, I decided to add more services so my clients could own and feel their worth, add value to the marketplace, and receive wealth for the value that they're adding to the marketplace *and* have a place to invest their money. This allows them to reduce their tax burden and have a plan for when they're older so they don't have to work so hard.

What is one of the most valuable lessons you've learned as an entrepreneur?

The most valuable lesson I've learned on my entrepreneurial journey has been valuing myself at a high level. The more I value myself, the more others will value me. I value myself by spending time with myself, charging what I'm worth, and surrounding myself with people who value me.

Spending time with myself is a key component of valuing myself. I spend time nourishing myself with healthy food and supplements to support my body. I spend time with myself exercising, practicing mindful movement, and meditating. I spend time with myself in nature. I spend time with myself in contemplation so that new ideas can rise from within, and entrepreneurial expansion happens through new ideas. I value myself by charging what I'm worth.

Oftentimes in the marketplace, when somebody starts a new business, others recommend they start at a low price point and work their way up to a higher price point. Unfortunately, this does not lead to sustainable revenue in a business. Unless somebody has a large following, big email list, or strong referral partnerships who can send them tons of people, very few people can sustain themselves by charging low and then charging high.

I started low when I first began my business. I charged less than $100 per hour and sold small packages. When I hired a private coach, I learned that I could sell high. I could start selling about five times what I already was and charge over $500 an hour. Once I started charging more, selling high-value packages, and pricing my services at a high level, I started attracting people worldwide who valued me at a high level.

So, my lesson is to go high and then go low. If you have many high-value clients, you can work on building your audience to a large number, whether that be on social media, email lists, referral partnerships, speaking, or whatever you're doing from a marketing standpoint. Once you have a large following, you can offer smaller programs and packages and lower-price services. But until you have a foundation of high-value clients, there's no need to sell low. If you're just starting out and you're 20 years old, then maybe you can start low. But if you have a lot of experience, go high. That's my biggest lesson.

The other lesson is surrounding myself with people who value me. I've had coaches and mentors the entire time I've been in business who cheer me on and believe in me, even when I didn't believe in myself. They've shown me how to fully trust and believe in myself. In my personal relationships, I surround myself with people who speak positively, who value themselves, and who show me unconditional love and value me. I make sure to listen to people who provide value. Building relationships is a key component of a successful business.

How have you and your business benefited from your involvement with Achieve Systems?

My business and I have benefited tremendously from being involved with Achieve Systems. When I met Robert Raymond, I thought to myself, "I don't know what Achieve is, but I'm willing to partner with this guy because of his powerful energy and clear vision."

With the support of Robert, Vanessa, the Achieve leadership team, and the members of the Achieve Systems community, I have had the opportunity to grow my revenue, create new business relationships and even be supported in my personal life endeavors. One of the best assets of Achieve are its members. I often tell people that Achieve is a community of heart-based leaders—the lovers of humanity—the "I just want to help people" people. There are so many people in the community who want to help you and refer you to people you can help.

The Achieve Conferences are the by far the best conferences to create leads for my business that I have ever attended. At the most recent conference, I came home with over sixty new leads! I have created over six-figures in revenue by partnering with Achieve Members and have been a guest speaker at over a dozen live and virtual Achieve events. Achieve has helped me add multiple revenue streams to my business, grow my team and helped me invent my first product. I love attending Achieve University every year to spark new ideas for my next level of business expansion.

One special thing about Achieve is their heart-based approach to business. I had a season of difficulty in my personal life and the leadership team showed me care, kindness, and compassion. They reached out to me to see how I was doing personally, not just in business. This meant more to me than any business support I could have ever been given. This true loving support deepened my trust and support of Achieve Systems even more.

Achieve Systems is a real business family with a plethora of safety nets to keep you feeling loved, supported, and seen. Just like families, the Achieve community sees each other often so we stay connected. The Achieve annual conferences are like family reunions; people love seeing each other every time! The monthly events, daily masterminds and super active Facebook community help me feel supported at all times, even as a solopreneur.

What does your morning routine look like?

I love my mornings. I'm very grateful to wake up with my sweetheart, B. A. Dallas. I wake up every morning with a smile on my face that I get to live another day in his presence. I drink a warm beverage—sometimes coffee, sometimes tea, sometimes lemon water—and allow myself to ease into the morning. I exercise, stretch, practice mindful movement, and open my body to prepare for the day.

Since I sit on a chair at the computer often, I want to make sure I feel good in my body before doing so. I cuddle and give love to my fifteen-year-old chihuahua, Speedy Gonzalez. I take him outside and get some sunshine on my face. I'm lucky to live in the mountains of Colorado; it's sunny almost every single day. I let that morning sunshine beat down on my face, warming my arms and legs and providing me with nourishment for

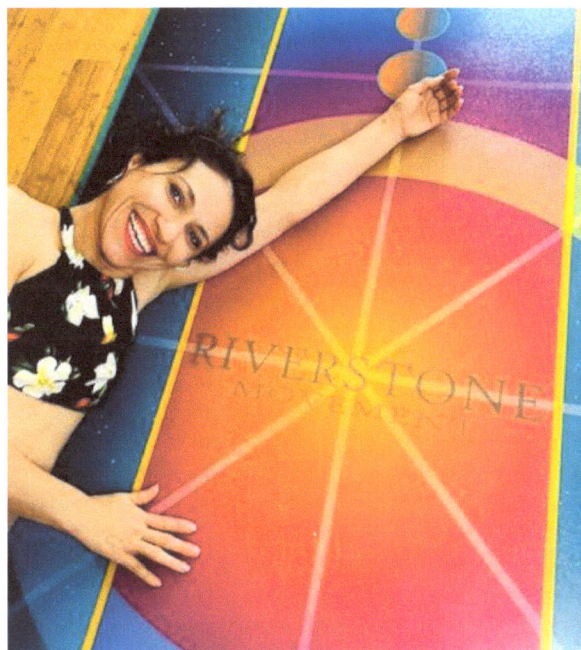

the day. Sometimes, I'm on my computer all day serving clients all around the world, so I might not see the sunshine in the middle of the afternoon. Thus, I make sure to get some of that morning sun.

I spend time with my sweetheart, talking about our lives. We talk about our vision for our life. We talk about what we're creating that day. And we talk about our ideas beyond business—what we're working on in our mind, what we're playing with in our creations. We listen to one another, share our ideas, and then suggest ideas to each other. It's more likely to occur when two or more are gathered for a common vision. And so, this morning time of envisioning our lives together and creating that vision together has led us to manifest more.

I also nourish myself with healthy food. I like to eat fruit and oatmeal in the mornings. I take supplements to nourish my body as well. I also get on social media and do some social media marketing after taking care of my body. I prefer feeling fresh in the morning on social media. I love Facebook; it has been a blessing to me. I'm grateful for the Internet. I respond to messages that I get on social media. And I cheer people on with the posts they put out in the mornings. I look through my memories from social media, from Facebook in particular, and see what I was up to a year ago, two years ago, four years ago. I reflect on how far I've come in such a short time. And then I nurture my community on social media.

So, nourishing myself, connecting with my sweetheart, exercising, meditating, and nourishing my community of like-minded clients, colleagues, and friends all around the world are some of my favorite activities in the morning.

What parting words of wisdom do you have for the reader?

If I could tell the readers anything, it would be to parent yourself in a way you wish you were parented. Even if you had fantastic parents, parent yourself even better. If you did not have fantastic parents, parent yourself just how you wish you had been. Mother yourself, father yourself. Be your own grandma. Be your own grandpa. Be the guide, the mentor, and the love that you deserve. Be that for yourself.

Own your worth. A parent finds their child worthy of love, gifts, and time. Speak kindly to yourself. The ideal parent speaks kind words to their children, speaks wisdom to their children, speaks love, speaks gently, and speaks firmly at times. Kindness to yourself is what you deserve. Thinking positively about yourself is what you deserve. That's what a strong parent does. They think kindly of their children. And you can think kindly of yourself, even if your parents didn't. If your parents did think kindly of you, mimic them. Use them as an example to treat yourself well and nourish yourself.

Nourish yourself with healthy, consistent food and drink. Never starve yourself. Never overindulge. Nourish yourself in a healthy way, just like a strong parent would do. Nourish yourself with gifts to celebrate. Celebrate yourself. When you have a win, celebrate. When you enroll a new client, make a new business deal, do something courageous (like speak on a stage for the first time), celebrate yourself. Buy yourself flowers, give yourself gifts. Take yourself out for a fun activity. You deserve to be celebrated. You deserve to celebrate your wins, just like a parent would do.

Nourish yourself with good people. A strong parent would not let you hang out with troublemakers or those who could have a bad influence on you. So, don't surround yourself with people who are negative people or talk badly about you, down to you, or bad about someone else. Be around the people who are creating in the world, who are creating from new ideas and materials—who are creating love. Be around the people who have smiles on their faces, generous spirits in their hearts, and the people willing to show up for you.

Just like a parent would do, unconditionally love yourself. Don't blame yourself. Don't shame yourself. Don't talk bad about yourself—ever. Not to yourself or to any other person. Don't use sarcasm. Be real, real, *real* loving to yourself. Be your own mother. Be your own father. Be your own grandmother and grandfather in the most ideal way possible.

Action Steps

1. **Implement embodiment practices:** After reading the article, consider incorporating embodiment and mindful movement into your daily routine. The author emphasizes that aligning your mind and body not only improves your self-worth but also positively impacts your business. Start with simple exercises to become more aware of your body and emotions, and gradually make it a regular part of your day.

2. **Reevaluate your pricing strategy:** The author suggests that one of the key aspects of owning your worth is charging what you're worth. Take a close look at your current pricing model and evaluate whether it truly reflects the value you bring to your clients. If necessary, restructure

your pricing to align with the high-value offers you provide, ensuring that you're not just competing on price but on the quality and value you deliver.

3. **Create an investment plan:** The third pillar the author discusses is the importance of investing in yourself. After generating wealth through your business, it's crucial to have a plan for that money. Consult with a financial mentor to explore investment opportunities that align with your long-term goals, both personal and professional. This will not only help you grow your wealth but also provide a safety net for the future.

About the Author

As a speaker, coach and CEO of The Riverstone Movement School, Lila Veronica helps high-performers, business owners and organizational leaders own their worth, work with high-end clients, and shift the physical component of their lives. She integrates mindfulness and movement into the business-mastery journey so her clients reach a greater potential faster without stressing or burning out. Through her speeches, programs, retreats, and collaborations with other thought leaders, Lila has personally mentored leaders on all seven continents to value themselves more, move mindfully, radically grow their revenue and increase their global impact.

FROM ELECTRICAL ENGINEER TO BUSINESS TRAILBLAZER

PHYLLIS MARLENE BENSTEIN

Choose a story from your childhood that you feel was important in becoming who you are today.

My mom was always my hero. My mom was a registered nurse. My family included my mom and dad and my brother, who was five years older than me. My mother took a job as the night supervisor at a local nursing home instead of working daytime in a hospital. She would go to work at 11:00 p.m. She got dropped off by my dad, worked all night, and was there in the morning for us to make breakfast and get us off to school, and then slept all day. She woke up before we got home from school, played with us for a while, spent time with us, made dinner for us, took a short nap, and then the whole thing started over again.

This story stands out in my mind because my mom was my hero. However, more importantly than that, she taught me at a very, very early age that you can have it all. You can have a successful career and be a wife and mom, and there's a way to juggle it all. That instilled in me a love of family and a family-first mentality. My mother changed her career, timing, and where she worked to be an incredible mom.

The other thing my mom taught me was work ethic. She showed me to never give up what you're passionate about, which for my mom was nursing. That has always stuck with me. From the time I was about five years old, I knew that I could be anything I wanted to be, and I would be fearless and unstoppable. I'd be able to have a family. I'd be able to have a full-time career.

My dad was also very influential. He was a mathematician. He worked during the day but then covered when my mom wasn't there. They showed me the importance of a great marriage. They showed the importance of teamwork, making it work, putting family first, and working hard to put a roof over our heads and food on the table. That's what I instilled in my kids: that I could be that mom. I was an engineer when I was raising my kids, and I showed them from a very early age how to be self-sufficient and how to be able to juggle it all.

What inspired you to start your business?

I'm a people person who's always loved connecting with others and connecting others to people and resources they want and need. My background is in electrical engineering, where I had a successful twenty-five-year career before I became an entrepreneur. One day, just a few years into my career, a female coworker asked me if I wanted to go with her to a professionals meeting for local women in business. I fell in love instantly with the casual atmosphere and being there with the purpose of meeting others. I joined that group and sought other opportunities to be in groups, where I excelled in the art of connecting and supporting others.

When the opportunity arose, I led my own chapter. I also learned early in my career that networking with my peers and management was the key to advancement. When the opportunity knocked at my door again with Achieve to own a networking brand, I jumped at this golden opportunity. Now, I help entrepreneurs, business owners, speakers, and authors be leaders and build community. I offer a master networking certification to teach others how to network with a purpose and monetize it.

I transformed my businesses into a reality by sharpening my ax (skill set). I led several women's networking groups for over a decade and learned from them everything about structures, how to fill seats, retain members, and be an inspirational leader. I also learned how to show up and build community with the local businesses.

In 2022, I had the opportunity to enhance my leadership and business ownership and develop and grow the networking arm of Achieve, the Connect and Collaboration Event System.

Another part of my business is clean beauty, self-care and wellness, stemming from allergies and looking for clean, nontoxic products. I've grown a successful and lucrative global ecommerce business. I educate worldwide about toxin awareness, providing people solutions for their haircare, skincare, and wellness needs, with an emphasis on aging gracefully and safely through clean practices and choices. This part of my business creates additional opportunities for lead generation through networking, speaking, and resources and products for entrepreneurs to look good, feel good, be and stay healthy.

Who are some key influences or mentors who played a role in your entrepreneurial journey?

Of course, it all started with my mom and the work ethic, drive, and leading by example she showed me. Many years later, one of my business partners, Toni Vanschoyck, became a vital mentor for me. She is also a wealth consultant. I'm working on my second network marketing company with her. She is highly successful and inspirational and leads by example. She showed me how to be a servant leader, love your people, work your business like a business, and dream bigger and then even bigger. She also mentored me on how to get paid what you are worth, protect your assets, and have diversity with multiple streams of income.

I don't work any of my businesses like a network marketing business. I learned from her about how to use it as a vehicle to change lives. My clean beauty business and networking business are all about how I can serve people. How can I make an impact and a difference? How can I mentor other people to make a difference? And that's what she has shown me all along—how to think outside the box.

She also taught me to play on my strong points and get help with my weaknesses; that's been huge for me. She helped with the systemization part of my business as well. We've done different product lines, but it's all about using those as a vehicle to solve people's problems, add additional revenue streams, and help them look and feel great.

Another great mentor for me is Robert Raymond, CEO and founder of Achieve Business Systems. I met Rob a few years ago, and what an impact he has made. His mind is brilliant. Everything he does is systematic and organized, and the community he has built has given me a community to thrive in. He's given me roadmaps. His endless resources are incredible. He's helped me develop things that weren't even on my radar before. His success over the past thirty years speaks volumes. Again, I resonate with people who have a true servant's heart and are doing the work and leading by example.

He's helped me build a seven-figure business with a seven-spoke ninja and taught me how to get it organized to get it done. Another big thing he helped me with was getting my book done. He has a simple process, well, not simple, but easy process for writing books. He sends you four packets, and you do a deep dive. You answer those four packets, and he sends you the template to write a book. My book, *The Journey from Employee to Entrepreneur*, had been in the works for a long time and was completed with his guidance. His experience, knowing what works and what doesn't work, was instrumental in helping me get it done. And just that community that keeps giving with all its resources, connections, and opportunities.

What makes your business unique and valuable?

My business is unique in that it encompasses a total approach for entrepreneurs and small business owners to start, grow, and sustain a business through lead generation opportunities I offer, as well as the clean living and image part. Being a successful leader and networking require making a lasting first impression and stepping out in public with class and style. Be memorable by developing your unique style as part of the complete package.

How does it address a specific need or solve a particular problem? I've been there. I was a successful electrical engineer in corporate America. I realized early in my career that my success and the success of others was from a combination of three things: verbal and nonverbal communication, your image (branding), and networking. I address a full-circle solution, making it a one-stop shop while addressing the needs that corporate employees, entrepreneurs, business owners, speakers, authors, and even those desiring to go from corporate to entrepreneurship have. My book, *The Journey from Employee to Entrepreneur*, has a roadmap and resources beyond that to help people.

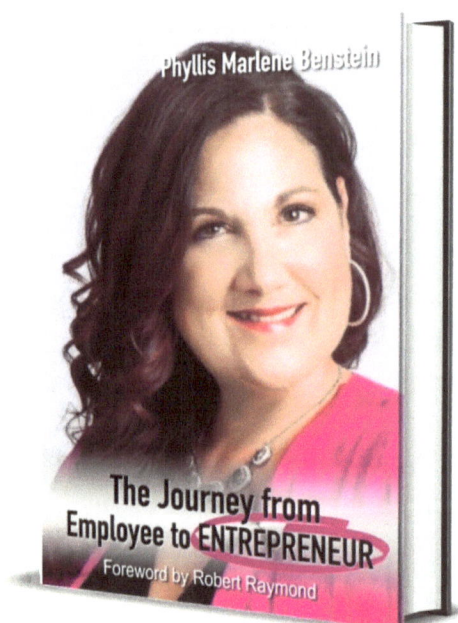

My book helps you to rediscover your "why," monetize your passions, and learn how to live, lead, and leave your legacy. Add to that the opportunities for lead generation and looking great to put it all together, not to mention there are revenue streams in all parts of my business. Many people fail at networking. Through Achieve, I've also developed a networking certification course called *Networking with a Purpose* that teaches others to become powerful connectors, making those key connections that convert. Overall, I'm unique in my full-circle, total approach to being a successful entrepreneur or business owner.

What is a valuable lesson you've learned as an entrepreneur?

Never, ever settle for less than you really want or deserve. It started when I was little. My dad was a mathematician. He drilled me on my math tables while riding around in the car. He also said he wouldn't pay for my college education unless I went into a technical field. But my mother had a love of the arts that she instilled in me. She had me in piano lessons at a very early age. I was a ballerina. I went to modeling school, and there was always a yin and yang inside me.

I ended up going to engineering school. I had a very successful twenty-five-year career as an electrical engineer. But that's not what I wanted deep down in my heart. That's not what fueled me. That's not what lit me up. I was a math whiz. That career was fun, but I wasn't ready to settle for less than I wanted or deserved. And I truly believe that everyone has a dream in their heart. Everyone has something that lights them up. Everyone has something they're good at and want to share with the world to make a difference.

I was stuck in the four walls of corporate day in and day out. I was sitting behind a desk making someone else money or successful. But I knew I couldn't settle, which became my mantra: Do not settle for less than you really want or deserve.

I found a way to make it happen. I advanced through the ranks in my corporate career. I built a toolbox. From day one of those twenty-five years, I started building a toolbox of interpersonal skills, communication skills, verbal and nonverbal communication skills, and networking. The technical part came easily to me. It was the people part I needed to work on. In corporate America, it was about management. I wanted to be a leader. I started a women's networking group while I was in corporate. And when the time arose, I took my toolbox and turned it into a business.

I hope others will never settle for less than they really want or deserve because there's always a way. But you have to have a plan. You have to have an exit strategy. That's why I wrote the book *The Journey from Employee to Entrepreneurs*. It ties it all together. So, if you're unhappy or don't think you're doing what you deserve to do or want, there is always a way to make a plan B or sometimes a plan C. I'm living proof that you can do that.

How have you and your business benefited from your involvement with Achieve Systems?

Thanks to my involvement with Achieve Systems, I have been able to transform my business into a million-dollar model. Working closely with the Robert and Vanessa Raymond and Achieve I was able to align my business model with my core values, beliefs, dreams, and life goals. This alignment not only gave me a strong sense of purpose and fulfillment but also attracted a loyal customer base and followers who resonate with my brand's message.

Moreover, Achieve Systems provided me with the tools and knowledge to diversify my offerings. Through their guidance, I successfully wrote and published my book, *The Journey from Employee to Entrepreneur*, Additionally, I wrote and published a networking certification, and co-authored a networking book. All of this has helped make me an industry authority, opening the door to numerous speaking engagements sponsorship opportunities, and business relationships and transactions. Being part of the Achieve Systems community has exposed me to a group of high-level successful individuals, providing me with endless inspiration and opportunities to show up for further growth and collaboration with like-minded entrepreneurs.

What does your morning routine look like?

I have a great morning routine, and I truly feel that what you do in the morning sets you up for the whole day. It's all about when I wake up and not picking up my phone or logging onto my computer first thing in the morning. First, I try to wake up and see the sunrise. I'm into the beauty of the sunrise, which starts my gratitude for the day. I have two locations, either facing the front range of the Rockies or being down the street from the beach in Florida. In Florida, I get up early and make sure that I am walking in town or on the beach for the sunrise. Then, I practice gratitude and acknowledge what I'm grateful for, taking in the sights and sounds. Wherever I am, I center myself, grounding myself for the day.

I then go over what my perfect day would be. I look at my schedule for the day, and I go through everything in my schedule, thinking about what the perfect outcome would be. I also try to get my exercise in early with that walk. Depending on the weather and temperature, it's a wide range between 5,000 and 10,000 steps. This has worked well for me. Sometimes, if the weather is not good and I'm inside, I use that time to write in my gratitude journal. My journaling includes

what my perfect day is, what my perfect life is, what I'm going to manifest, and what I want to bring into my life. This focuses and grounds me and sets up a day that can't go bad because it started with intention and gratitude.

What parting words of wisdom do you have for the reader?

You got this. Have unshakable belief, determination, perseverance, grit, and, of course, bounce-back ability. If at first you don't succeed, try, try again. And follow your heart and your dreams. Use your God-given gifts and talents to create your best life and highest version of yourself so that you can live, lead, and leave your legacy.

Action Steps

1. **Reevaluate your networking strategy:** Inspired by the author's journey, consider how you can better leverage networking to advance your business. Whether it's joining a local business group, attending industry events, or even starting your own networking chapter, make a plan to actively engage with peers, mentors, and potential clients.

2. **Diversify your offerings:** The author didn't limit herself to one avenue of business; she expanded into clean beauty and wellness alongside her networking endeavors. Take a moment to think about how you can diversify your business offerings to reach a wider audience and add multiple revenue streams.

3. **Invest in skill development:** The author emphasized the importance of "sharpening her ax," or continually improving her skill set. Identify areas where you could enhance your skills, whether it's leadership, marketing, or product development, and consider taking courses or certifications to level up your expertise.

About the Author

Phyllis Marlene Benstein is a visionary and master connector with a diverse background in engineering, corporate America leadership, makeup artistry, toxin awareness and image consulting. She is the Director of Networking and Community with Achieve Systems and through her networking brand "Connect & Collaborate" she provides entrepreneurs with global opportunities to speak, sponsor, attend events, and even become chapter owners. With her unique blend of expertise and a passion for transformation, Phyllis Marlene helps others go from ordinary to extraordinary by building powerful relationships and helping them enhance their image and personal brand. She is dedicated to serving others and empowering them to be their true and highest version of themselves. Connect with Phyllis Marlene at phyllismarlene.com.

SKYROCKET YOUR CONNECTION IQ

WITH MASTER
CONNECTOR PHYLLIS
MARLENE BENSTEIN

LET'S CONNECT:

Catalog

NETWORKING
With a Purpose
CERTIFICATION

LET'S UP-LEVEL YOUR AUDIENCE & INCREASE YOUR TRANSACTIONS!

WHAT'S INCLUDED?

- DEFINING & FIND YOUR TARGET AUDIENCE
- HOW TO SHOW UP AND MAKE A LASTING IMPRESSION
- AN EXTENSIVE BREAKDOWN OF PLACES TO NETWORK
- DON'T JUST "NETWORK"
- SUCCESSFUL MESSAGING TECHNIQUES WITH TRACKING AND CONVERTING YOUR LEADS
- DEFINING UNIQUE SELLING PROPOSITION (USP)
- BUILDING RAPPORT AND ESTABLISHING TRUST
- CREATING YOUR GAME PLAN TO ACHIEVE YOUR

- –WALK INTO EVERY EVENT WITH A PROFIT EXPECTATION AND PLAN (CREATED RIGHT IN THE WORKSHOP)
- LEARN TO SHOW UP WITH A GOAL IN MIND TO MAKE BIG MONEY AND CREATE HIGH-LEVEL WIN-WIN RELATIONSHIPS
- WITH THE RIGHT PEOPLE!

NEED LEADS?
COME AND NETWORK
WITH US

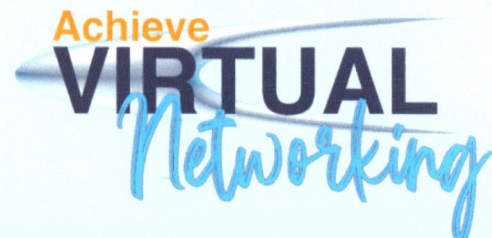

REGISTER AT:
CONNECTANDCOLLABORATE.CO

CONNECT WITH PHYLLIS:
PHYLLIS@PHYLLISMARLENE.COM